The
Inclusion Revolution
Is Now

The Inclusion Revolution Is Now

*An Innovative Framework for Diversity
and Inclusion in the Workplace*

Maura G. Robinson, MPA

iUniverse LLC
Bloomington

THE INCLUSION REVOLUTION IS NOW
AN INNOVATIVE FRAMEWORK FOR DIVERSITY
AND INCLUSION IN THE WORKPLACE

iUniverse books may be ordered through booksellers or by contacting:

iUniverse
1663 Liberty Drive
Bloomington, IN 47403
www.iuniverse.com
1-800-Authors (1-800-288-4677)

Because of the dynamic nature of the Internet, any web addresses or links contained in this book may have changed since publication and may no longer be valid. The views expressed in this work are solely those of the author and do not necessarily reflect the views of the publisher, and the publisher hereby disclaims any responsibility for them.

Any people depicted in stock imagery provided by Thinkstock are models, and such images are being used for illustrative purposes only. Certain stock imagery © Thinkstock.

ISBN: 978-1-4917-1057-9 (sc)
ISBN: 978-1-4917-1056-2 (hc)
ISBN: 978-1-4917-1058-6 (e)

Library of Congress Control Number: 2013918777

Printed in the United States of America.

iUniverse rev. date: 10/18/2013

I dedicate this book to Mark, Olivia, Bobbie, and Bonnie

Table of Contents

Introduction..ix

Chapter 1   Civic Diversity versus Organizational Diversity: The
            Inclusion Revolution Framework 1

Chapter 2   Top Management Support in a Systemic approach
            to Diversity and Inclusion 7

Chapter 3   Three Different Models of Diversity Practices................. 11

Chapter 4   A Logic Model as a Tool.. 17

Chapter 5   Inclusion Management Competencies for Systemic
            Approach to Change 25

Chapter 6   Why Disproportionality Has a Great Impact in a
            Systemic Process of Change 29

Chapter 7   The Generational Impact on a Systemic Process of
            Change.. 35

Chapter 8   The Impact of Unconscious Bias in a Systemic Pro-
            cess of Change 43

Chapter 9   Diversity and Inclusion Readiness Assessment Tool........ 51

Chapter 10 The Power of Diverse Groups in a Systemic Pro-
            cess of Change 57

Chapter 11 Professional Development for the Success of a
            Systemic Process of Change 65

Chapter 12 The Diversity and Inclusion Professional......................... 69

Chapter 13 Accountability 75

Chapter 14 Best Practices for Diversity and Inclusion...................... 79

Chapter 15 A Systemic Approach to Diversity and Inclusion at
            Its Best 83

Conclusion.. 87

Works Cited 89

Introduction

I became a sociologist because I have always been intrigued by different cultures and how they interact in society. I also found it fascinating how many cultures exist in the workplace and how each of them interact to meet the company's bottom line. In 1990 I returned to school to get my master's degree in public administration so I could open a company specializing in diversity and inclusion in the workplace. I have over twenty-six years of experience in corporate America, and my company M. G. Robinson, Inc. has been in existence for the last twenty years.

I was inspired to write this book after I designed a framework for diversity and inclusion that I was utilizing for my professional development sessions for corporations. I noticed that when I unveiled my systemic approach of change to employees, they were taken back but very responsive to what I was sharing with them. In many cases employees would tell me that for the very first time, they understood what diversity and inclusion meant for them in the workplace. Even individuals who didn't want to be in the sessions were captivated by the behavioral approach to diversity and inclusion that I was sharing with them. I designed this framework because I was tired of hearing the same civic diversity material telling me over and over again that diversity was the right thing to do or that diversity was about the struggles of a group.

The more I researched and studied diversity models and worked with the different corporations, the more I learned about the need for management and employees to understand that diversity was not a feeling but a behavior in action. I also found the need for corporations to know how to apply new behaviors for tangible cultural changes within the workplace.

In 2010, the latest year for which data are available, white women earned 78.1 percent on the dollar compared to white men; African American women earned 89.8 percent compared to black men; Hispanic women earned 91.3 percent compared to Hispanic men, and Asian women earned 79.7 percent compared to Asian men. The wage gap is lower for black and Latino women in part because wages for people of color tend to be lower overall. This gap occurs within racial/ethnic groups as well. In 2010, according to the Census Bureau, African Americans earned only 58.7 percent of what whites earned, while Hispanics earned only 69.1 percent of what whites earned. The American Association of University Women tackled the pay gap by looking at workers of the same educational attainment—same kind of education, holding the same kinds of jobs, and having made the same choices about marriage and number of kids. They found that college-educated women earn 5 percent less the first year out of school than their male peers. Ten years later, even if they keep working on par with those men, the women earn 12 percent less (Glynn 2013).

As we look at the data reflecting the disparity within the workforce, a systemic process of change through my framework helps organizations understand the steps they must follow to succeed in creating a culture of inclusion.

I would be remiss if I didn't acknowledge that there is still racism, prejudice, sexism, and other exclusionist attitudes among people in the workplace, but what I'm trying to show with my framework in this book is that at the organizational level, the leadership has the power and the responsibility to mandate a climate of inclusion by putting in place a systemic process of change. The message of accountability and support from the leadership of the organization must embody what inclusion looks like through a behavioral approach to change. What I propose with my framework is a new way to adopt diversity and inclusion practices within the workplace by hiring, retaining, and promoting individuals from the culture of difference. Let's face it, most diversity practices used by organizations right now do not actually promote inclusion, thus exclusion continues to exist.

My revolutionary framework on diversity and inclusion is a systemic process that is divided in two prongs. One is the employee awareness or the "I," and the other is the organizational achievement component, or the "we." The first prong comprises the total support of the leadership team and works with each employee at each different level of the organization to help him or her understand what a behavioral systemic approach means, and how it affects each and every person he or she comes in contact with at the organizational level. The second prong of my framework is the organizational achievement phase, or the "we." At this phase the "we" addresses the question, "How do we work together to impact tangible change related to inclusion?"

During this phase of the creating and incorporation of a systemic process of change for diversity and inclusion, the core values of the organization dictate what work is required. For this book, I will concentrate on defining the first prong of my framework—the "I."

One of the main reasons I am writing this book is because I believe that organizations at all levels have the responsibility and the power to create a culture of inclusion within their workforces, and that they are able to eliminate disparity gaps and promote a climate of inclusion where diverse and non-diverse employees work together to meet the organizational goals.

Please read this book with an open mind and go through the whole book a couple of times if necessary to get the full sense of the framework. If you are used to the feeling (civic diversity) approach to diversity in the workplace, it may take some time to get used to the behavioral aspect of the systemic approach that I sharing with you.

I hope that this book inspires you to create a difference. Use this book as a reference and a guide to create a culture of inclusion in your organization. Remember that leadership support is a must and that the ability to communicate the systemic process of change to all employees is essential. This systemic process of change only works if every employee within the organization follows the practices of change to create a culture of inclusion.

Chapter 1

Civic Diversity versus Organizational Diversity: The Inclusion Revolution Framework

As a sociologist and a business woman, I have always been fascinated by the behavioral aspect of cultures. I have always been intrigued by the way people act and react and how those attributes influence human behavior. This thirst for knowledge has helped me embark on the research and understanding of cultures in a different dimension and how they affect people within the workplace. The way diversity is typically introduced and practiced at the organizational level does not create a long standing systemic process of inclusion that transforms organizations into excellence driven organization. (See chapter 9, "Diversity and Inclusion Readiness Assessment.")

As I work with organizations in helping them create a culture of inclusion, I find two common denominators that impede them from creating a sustainable, systemic process of change. The first one is the belief that diversity and inclusion only relates to color, race, gender, etc., and that the efforts to create a culture of inclusion is focused in how these selected groups are accepted within the workforce. Secondly, most organizations utilize "civic diversity" as daily practice, and have a strategic diversity plan that is also based on "civic diversity."

Civic diversity refers to the assumption that the best way to sensitize employees at the organizational level regarding diversity is through the sharing of the struggles of a culture that has been oppressed in the past or is perceived to continue to be oppressed in the present. This type of approach to diversity and inclusion is not effective at the workplace because it does not create a systemic change within the organization. Employees cannot and will not understand or implement inclusion through civic diversity because the way they feel about diversity or the culture of difference is part of their own belief system. In some cases the civic approach to diversity and inclusion creates more disparity within the organization than change. Under civic diversity ideology, the individual is responsible for driving the climate of change. Inclusion is left to each individual to achieve, police, and implement. The organization takes a hands-off approach and only gets involved in diversity issues at the punitive level.

For instance, stop any of the employees in your organization right now and ask him or her what diversity means to him or her within the workplace. Most answers will be vague. You will hear, "It is the right thing to do," "It is important to respect others differences," or "I don't know." Civic diversity is very unclear to employees because there are no tangible guidelines of conduct or behavioral expectations from employees.

The worst diversity training I have ever attended had a facilitator who thought that civic diversity was the way to sensitized employees at the workplace. In one of his exercise he showed pictures of people of color and then asked the participants to identify who they thought was a professional and who was a criminal. Once the participants came up with their answers, the facilitator shamed them for their answers and preached to them about racial profiling. Half of the participants left the training at break time.

Diversity and inclusion at the organizational level are the behaviors we exhibit every time we come in contact with another human being and the way we choose to interact with that individual. Regardless of our own implicit and unconscious biases, our behavior will determine if the interaction is a positive or negative experience for both the communicator and the listener. (See chapter 8 on unconscious and implicit biases.)

Diversity is not a feeling; it is a behavior in action. The behavior can be negative or positive. Organizational diversity is a systematic, behavioral process of change that is driven by upper management, followed and understood by each employee regardless of his or her own personal beliefs, and is implemented by the whole organization to create and manage a culture of inclusion. So the concept of diversity moves from a feeling that has no intentional purpose to a functional, systemic mind-set of tangible change. Diversity is the notion and inclusion is the motion; in other words, organizational diversity is the function of creating and sustaining a culture of inclusion.

Diversity or inclusion at the organizational level is not a thing, or a person or a department. It is everything an employee does when he or she comes in contact with another human being at the workplace. It goes beyond race, color, gender, disability, or sexual orientation, etc.

My approach focuses on the behaviors related to diversity and inclusion to improve the cultural climate of an organization and also helps employees stay employed by sharing with them how to utilize and follow the organizational competencies designed by the organization. The main objective is for employees to learn behavioral aspects of diversity and inclusion that exist every time they come in contact with a coworker. The intangible feeling of diversity as a mind-set becomes a tangible performance outcome for each employee. (Performance outcome is what a learner has to do to demonstrate competence.) Because pay increases, promotions, recruitment, and retention of a diverse workforce are part of performance appraisal, he or she understands accountability, and thus diversity and inclusion practices are part of each work day. Organizations that have a strong systemic approach to change have checks, balances, and procedures in place to prevent any type of human abuse such as sexual harassment and/or sexual abuse, because the leadership and the workforce understand that diversity and inclusion are integral parts of a healthy, functional organization. History has shown that within organizations where there is dominance of a gender, race, or religion, etc., individuals may have a false sense of power and dominance over others. The sex scandals of the Catholic Church and the armed forces are perfect examples of such dysfunctional entities.

The most common concept of diversity is understood as the right thing to do (civic diversity), instead of the smart, behavioral approach adopted at the organizational level to help organizations survive in a global economy. In order for organizations to meet their bottom line, they must look at the whole composition of the workforce and how employees work together to accomplish their organizational goals.

There is an erroneous belief that if equity policies to manage diversity are written, inclusion will be present and practiced by all employees. The fact is that these policies are a camouflage, in some cases, to the true practice of inclusion. The word *equity* gives an illusion of inclusion within the workplace. When it comes to diverse populations, employment, retention, and promotion are not the same at the organizational level. Equity is defined as challenging discrimination, removing barriers faced by people from different groups, and creating a fairer society where everyone can participate and has the same opportunities to fulfill their potential. Unless a systemic behavioral approach is put in place at the organizational level, inclusion cannot be part of the group's culture. Diversity must be a behavior in action that dictates the actions of all employees within the workplace and is part of everything they do while at work. It is through behavior modification at the organizational level that companies can create long lasting systemic changes and a culture of inclusion.

Policies that describe respect and equality in the workplace do not relate any tangible knowledge to employees, but organizational competencies that are linked with accountability standards help dictate the behavior expected by each employee and the organizational commitment to diversity and inclusion.

Human capital is so very valuable and important to organizations. These individuals are the ones that make institutions succeed or fail. Each employee must understand that his or her ability to work with others, regardless of his or her own personal beliefs, helps meet the bottom line and promote a culture of inclusion. Then, the behavioral approach to diversity and inclusion becomes the responsibility of each employee within the organization. The organization then demands[1] the behaviors of success to achieve inclusion as an organizational goal. Organizations are used to making demands to its employees such as being on time, following dress codes, and observing safety rules so implementing a behavior of inclusion should not be an exception.

My revolutionary framework on diversity and inclusion has a systemic process that is divided in two prongs. One is the employee's awareness or the "I" and the other is the organizational component or the "we." The first prong has the total support of the leadership team and works with each employee at each different level of the organization to help him or her understand what a behavioral systemic approach means and how it affects each and every one he or she comes in contact with. For the first time, the employee has a concrete, experiential, and tangible understanding of diversity and inclusion. Then he or she learns that organizational competencies are designed to help map his or her behavior and how, by following those competencies, it creates employment sustainability. The expectations of a behavior of acceptance are now set forth by the organization to help meet its bottom line, and thus working for a company becomes a rental agreement between an employee and the

---

[1] (Ramarajan 2008)

company. The acceptance of a paycheck signifies that the employee is renting out his or her services, talents, and skills to a company, so the company can meet its bottom line. Once the employee understands that he has been hired to meet the tangible goals of productivity for his company, the creating and management of a culture of inclusion affirms the understanding of the behaviors expected from him or her, so he or she is no longer allowed to bring personal feelings of exclusion to the workplace.

The table below will show you how the systemic platform is set up to introduce first prong—the "I"—to the organization. The question asked is, "How do I fit in within the organization?" Each department is introduced to the systemic process of change separately, so individual departments learn how the organizational competencies impact them and how to use them to create a culture of inclusion. The commitment of the leadership team and intentional purpose will help the organization to achieve its organizational goals. (See the section on professional development to understand how each element of the structure of prong I works.)

This first book is primarily based on my framework prong I.

Organizational Diversity

Systemic Platform of Change Prong I

Employee Awareness – The "I"

Based on organizational Competencies

A Culture of Inclusion starts to emerge

The Opportunity Creators

Staying Employee	Supplier Development	Maintaining a healthy workforce	Finding the talent	Retaining the workforce	Harvesting the talent/ Selecting the best	Growing & Developing the Business
↓	↓	↓	↓	↓	↓	↓
First Level Employees	Procurement	Human Resources		Recruitment Admissions	Managers Supervisors	VPs, CEOs, Board of Directors, Trustees, Foundation Director.

*How do I fit in within the organization?
*Driven by Upper Management
*Intentional Purpose is introduced

Note: This organization structure may be different for educational and service settings.

The second prong of my framework is the organizational achievement phase or the "we." The question asked at this phase is, "How do we work together to impact tangible change related to inclusion?"

During this phase of the creation and incorporation of a systemic process for change, the core values of the organization dictate what work is necessary. At this phase a culture of inclusion is practiced by all, and a sense of community emerges. The employees now come together from the different departments to take part in creating tangible changes. The question becomes how "we" can sustain a culture of inclusion and incorporate the organizational core values in every facet of our work and within the organization. The success of this part of the systemic process is the responsibility of hiring managers, human resource officers, and the action council of the organization. The mission of these individuals is to make coworkers accountable for their behavior, so they continue the ground work, and the culture of inclusion becomes weaved into every facet of the organization.

The following diagram describes prong II of my framework.

Organizational Diversity
Systemic Platform of Change Prong II
Organizational Achievement – The "We"
Based on organizational Core Value

A culture of Inclusion is the practice

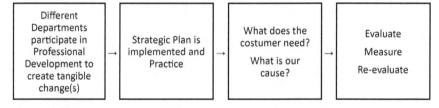

| Different Departments participate in Professional Development to create tangible change(s) | → | Strategic Plan is implemented and Practice | → | What does the costumer need?

What is our cause? | → | Evaluate

Measure

Re-evaluate |

The biggest challenge is organizational Unconscious behaviors – biases

*How do we work together to impact tangible change related to Inclusion?

*Each one of us is responsible for creating a culture of Inclusion

*Driven by Action Council, HR and Hiring Managers.

My systemic process for diversity and inclusion takes time to implement because of its numerous components. It is also an ongoing process, because systemic processes are always evolving. It is the need for continuous evaluation to adjust or improve that makes this process solid.

Chapter 2

Top Management Support in a Systemic approach to Diversity and Inclusion

The following chapters explain the different components of my framework: prong I, the "I," to illustrate the success of its implementation at the organizational level. Top management support is one of the first requirements in creating a shared vision for a systemic change; this change, in turn, establishes a high value for helpful human behavior. Positive and lasting behavioral change is the primary advantage of the culture change approach. Change agents must determine how new behavior will become a strategic advantage for the success of the organization.

For too many years diversity and inclusion at the organizational level have been regarded as separate concerns. The diversity component is addressed mostly by someone from a culture of difference, and the primary goal of this person or department is to fix all the "diversity issues" the organization may have. The reality is that it takes the top leadership of an organization to bridge the diversity gap. It is the vision and commitment of the top leadership team that allows employees to be immersed in a behavioral process of culture change within the workforce and then makes them responsible for addressing and creating a culture of inclusion.

The Visionary

It takes the president or CEO of a company to impose the behavior of diversity and inclusion, which must be implemented throughout the organization. This individual must have the vision, understanding, and intentional purpose to move the organization to a functional level of diversity and inclusion. This individual will make sure that his leadership team is on board and will become the ambassadors of the behavior, the message, and the practice of systemic inclusion.

The Leadership Team Implements the Foundation for Change

Members of the leadership team have the greatest impact in creating cultural change within the organization, because they supervise the majority of the employees that help meet the bottom line. For a culture of inclusion to exist at the organizational level, the leadership team must be on board with the systemic process for change; otherwise the intention to change becomes a program or an initiative and will be seen as simply a civic approach to diversity instead of a behavioral approach for systemic change.

Who is Part of the Top Leadership Team?

The president or chief financial officer, vice presidents, trustees and board of directors, and any group within the organization that has the power to impact policy all represent top leadership.

Moving Forward

The leadership team will be involved in the growth and development part of the inclusion revolution framework. This component of the framework will be addressed through the organizational competencies that help create the strategic plan to address employment and retention disparities related to race, gender, ethnicity, sexual orientation, and individuals with disabilities. This strategic plan will also emphasize hiring and promotion goals by using the employee population index instead of the community population index.

This group will also set up tangible purchasing goals (unless there are already federal or state mandates) for the organization that will include using certified minority- or women-owned businesses, veterans, and/or small business enterprises. A starting goal must be at least 10 to 15 percent of the total purchasing power of the organization to be directed toward these types of businesses.

How Would the Top Leadership Create a Culture of Inclusion?

The top leadership team will create and establish several systemic processes of engagement. The first one will be to develop a systemic approach to change through a logic-based model.

The second component will include a mentoring platform that will focus on ensuring that race, gender, ethnicity, sexual orientation, disabilities, and veteran status are part of the outreach process.

The third systemic process for developing a culture of inclusion will be a structure to help lead a multigenerational workforce.

All these processes will be driven by the core values of the organization, as well as the competencies for success that are developed by the organization.

My framework for the inclusion revolution will not create a culture of inclusion unless the top leadership team buys into it. Their support, behavior, commitment, and accountability are essential elements to the implementation of a systemic process of inclusion at the workplace.

Accountability within the Top Leadership Team

Accountability is achieved by making the top leadership team responsible for the inclusion management of the systemic process of change. It is necessary to link the success of the implementation of cultural change to the performance evaluation and compensation of the leadership team. Accountability also helps to ensure that everyone is on board and actively engaging in the ongoing systemic process of inclusion throughout the organization. See chapter 13 on accountability for specific tools and skills.

Chapter 3

Three Different Models of Diversity Practices

The common practice of civic diversity (see chapter on civic diversity vs. organizational diversity) is ineffective, and the structure of diversity and inclusion at the organizational level is mostly thought of as a program or an initiative. Implementing diversity and inclusion as programs or initiatives is dangerous because doing so will not actually create a culture of change within the workforce. My inclusion revolution framework looks at the impact of behavior within the workplace and how employees learn to modify their behavior in order to continue to be employed and to meet the bottom line. It is essential that employees understand that diversity and inclusion within the workplace are related to their ability to work with others regardless of their own personal beliefs.

The work of Bernardo M. Ferdman and Sari Einy Brody offers three different models on diversity. [2] Two of these models are still the most frequently used in the workplace in spite of being less effective, and the third one is a business model that reaffirms why my systemic approach to diversity is the best way to create an environment of inclusion at the organizational level.

The models are the moral imperative (or civic diversity) model, the legal and social pressures model, and the business success (organizational diversity) model.

---

[2] (Ferdman 2004)

The Moral Imperative or Civic Diversity Model

The notion of multiculturalism is relatively recent and is also the source of much contention. Diversity initiatives, or programs grounded in the moral imperative, typically adopt the notion that pluralism and multiculturalism are the best options for all individuals, groups, and societies in that they are likely to lead to the most positive outcomes. Multiculturalism means recognizing and valuing the range of cultural and other out group-based differences among people.[3] It also entails seeing these differences as providing essential contributions to society and therefore striving to eliminate invidious, ethnocentric comparisons, as well as finding ways to foster positive expression of the differences. Berr (1993)[4] and Cox and Finley-Nickelson (1991)[5] describe pluralism or integration as involving the coexistence in one society or organization of groups that differ along cultural lines, while maintaining distinct ethnic and cultural identities. Proponents of the moral imperative argue that it is incumbent on the beneficiaries of this historical pattern of oppression, discrimination, and bias to begin to truly level the playing field in a way more consistent with the values of liberty, equality, and justice. Leveling the playing field involves heightening awareness of these inequities and recognizing how the experiences of people of color and women have differed from those of white men. Thus, the desire to contribute to the development of a better society by doing the right thing can be an important motivation for diversity and inclusion.

The moral imperative or civic diversity and its variations are associated with particular visions of the ideal organization that are, in turn, related to the goals set for diversity initiatives and the criteria used to assess their effectiveness. Although proponents of the moral arguments for diversity initiatives often disagree as to whether the focus should be on reducing systemic oppression or on accepting and valuing the full range of human variation, they do agree that the ultimate emphasis must be on both individual and social change. In this model the organization is not part of the thought process; consequently the systemic process of change at the organizational level does not exist.

---

[3] (Katz 1989)
[4] (Berry 1993)
[5] (Cox 1991)

Legal and Social Pressures Model

Federal regulations and court rulings have forced organizations to face legal and social demands to become more inclusive, at least in numbers.[6] These regulations include equal employment opportunity (EEO) laws, affirmative action (AA), and the Americans with Disabilities Act (ADA). Businesses that enter into contracts with the federal government become subject to EEO/AA laws and regulations. Addressing sexual harassment has also become a prominent issue. More and more organizations realize they must take active steps to prevent lawsuits charging discrimination or harassment.

Whether or not organizations view addressing diversity as the right thing to do or as good for business, they frequently find themselves under legal pressure to do so. When motivated primarily by legal pressures, the focus of interventions is usually on specific groups. When motivated in this way, diversity initiatives tend to be focused more broadly and are less constrained by legal definitions of protected groups. Nevertheless, if the impetus is primarily external and framed solely in terms of special interests, it can be difficult for the organization to articulate clear and forceful arguments for starting and continuing the intervention, since the intervention speaks to all members of an organization and is perceived as intrinsically linked to the organization's best interests.

In some organizations, diversity initiatives have been implemented as part of consent agreements stemming from successful legal challenges to current practices. In such organizations, the initial motivation for diversity and inclusion is based chiefly on legal and social pressures and is thus reactive, rather than proactive.

When diversity initiatives are driven primarily by legal and social pressures, the concept of inclusion can become quite controversial because what is viewed from one group's perspective as an appropriate and fair measure taken to remedy inequalities within the group can be viewed by other groups as unfair, wrong, or divisive. Many diversity consultants argue that initiatives framed solely from this perspective are much less likely to be successful in the long term, because they encounter more resistance from members of groups that do not feel included or believe they have something to lose—white males in particular.[7]

---

[6] (Cox 1993)
[7] (Gardenswartz, 1993)
(Solomon 1993)

Business Success and Competitiveness or
Inclusion Revolution Model

At the organizational level the model that has the most impact in creating diversity and inclusion is this model. This model is expected to impact employees' behavior, business success and the bottom line. As viewed from this perspective, increasing globalization and a more diverse domestic workforce are "push" factors (i.e., organizations that do nothing will lose ground), whereas the benefits to be had from working effectively across different cultures are "pull" factors (i.e., organizations that take advantage will do better and more competitive).[8]

Research shows that the need not only to frame the business case for diversity but also to go beyond using it as a sales tool and to be as clear as possible about benefits that organizations can gain from becoming more inclusive.[9] These benefits include improvement in retention, skills performance, and development of employees; being better prepared to work with internal and external customers, partners, and suppliers and expanding the range of business opportunities within the marketplace; better business and quality of life for stakeholders in the community; and increased productivity and the capacity to deal with change effectively and creatively within the organization at large. The organization becomes the ideal place of employment for people in the community.

Inclusion from the vantage point of business success is about making sure the organization uses all productive capacity and potential to the full extent. If employees can be more effective, and if they believe is that diversity will help them become so, then the organization can also be more productive and successful, and diverse populations will have the opportunity to succeed along with the organization.

By valuing, encouraging, and ultimately including the full contributions of all members, organizations will have a broader range of talent available and will be much more likely to succeed in creating a culture of inclusion within the workplace.[10]

Thus, inclusion from the vantage point of business success is not limited to particular groups or categories of people. All individuals must be included in their full uniqueness and complexity. Doing this, however, also includes

---

[8] (Cox 1991)
(Jackson 1992)
[9] (Ibid.)
[10] (Miller 1994)

recognizing the group-based differences among people.[11] Moreover, once organizations learn to adopt an attitude of inclusivity in dealing with their members, this will also have a positive impact on how view their customer base, how they develop products and assess business opportunities, and how they relate to their communities.

This model of diversity and inclusion becomes a key strategy for organizational viability and effectiveness. In the same way that teams can be used as workplace design to bring about higher performance, diversity is used as a means to an end. The goal is to make the organization the best it can be. If this takes including more views, including a variety of people, empowering workers, and effecting social change, so be it, as long as the organization is more successful.

Because of this systems view, business success motivation is the most likely to lead to a strategic approach to diversity and inclusion, in which these two components have a long-term impact on organizational change.

The success of this systemic process of change model is measured in terms of movement toward both the full use of people and the accomplishment of organizational aims, including strategic objectives that go beyond the workforce.[12]

Now that all the different models on diversity have been explained, let's explore the importance of a systemic process of change in creating a culture of inclusion within the workplace. The different sections of this book will explain in detail why my framework on organizational diversity has such a great impact in creating a culture of inclusion at the workplace thus the inclusion revolution occurs.

---

[11] (Ferdman 1995)
[12] (Katz 1994)

Chapter 4

A Logic Model as a Tool

One of the first steps in creating a shared vision for a culture change is to establish a high value for helpful human behavior. Positive and lasting behavior change is the primary advantage of the culture change approach. Therefore, culture change leaders must determine how new behavior will become a strategic advantage to the success of the organization.

The cultural climate can help people feel connected and open to change in the workplace. Climate is felt through the sense of community, shared vision, and a positive outlook. These cultural qualities are imbedded in social interaction. When climate factors are noticeably absent, their development must become a part process for change,[13] so inclusion can occur, and the organization will be able to meet its bottom line. The importance of utilizing a systemic process for change to advance diversity and inclusion at the organizational level is that it permits employees to explore the talents and skills that others bring to the table regardless of who they are or from where they come.

A systemic approach is composed of many elements, and each element has a way to connect with each employee. I recommend using logic models to develop the different components of a systemic approach to diversity and inclusion.

A systemic approach to diversity and inclusion is an ongoing process that takes time to implement. It should be thought out and communicated to the staff at all levels of the organization via professional development and informal group meetings. The success of prong I and prong II of the

---

[13] (Allen 2008)

inclusion revolution depends on the awareness and the practice of the new behaviors by the staff.

What Is a Logic Model?

A logic model presents a picture of how your systemic approach is supposed to work. It explains why your strategy is a good solution to the problem at hand. Effective logic models make an explicit, often visual, statement of the activities that will bring about change and the results you expect to see for the community and its people at the organizational level. A logic model keeps participants moving in the same direction by providing a common language and point of reference.

More than an observer's tool, logic models become part of the work itself. They energize employees and rally support for change by declaring precisely what you're trying to accomplish and how.

A diversity and inclusion logic model supports the work of health promotion and organizational development by charting the course of workforce transformation as it evolves.

A logic model refers to "the relationship between elements and between an element and the whole." All of us have a great capacity to see patterns in complex phenomena. We see systems at work and find within them an inner logic a set of rules or relationships that govern behavior. Working alone, we can usually discern the logic of a simple system. And by working in teams, persistently over time if necessary, there is hardly any system, past or present, whose logic we can't decipher[14].

Why Develop a Logic Model?

Logic models have numerous uses and benefits. A logic model can be used for:

Strategic Planning: Developing a logic model is a form of strategic planning. The process forces you to identify your vision, the rationale behind your systemic change, and how your systemic change will work. This process is also a good way to get a variety of systemic stakeholders involved in planning and to build consensus on the systemic design and operations.

Effective Communication: Logic models allow you to provide a snapshot of your system and your intended outcomes to funders, staff, policymakers,

---

[14] (Horsch 1997)

the media, or other colleagues. They are particularly useful for incorporating diversity and inclusion as a way to show that what you are doing is strategic and that you have a plan for being accountable.

Evaluation Planning: A logic model provides the basic framework for an evaluation. It identifies the outcomes you seek based on your system of change and it puts those outcomes in measurable terms.

Continuous Learning and Improvement: A completed logic model provides a point of reference against which progress toward the achievement of desired outcomes can be measured on an ongoing basis.

Components of a Logical Model
A logic model ought to provide direction and clarity by presenting the big picture of change along with certain important details.

- **Purpose,** or mission: What motivates the need for change? This can also be expressed as the problems or opportunities that the system is addressing.

- **Context,** or conditions: What is the climate in which change will take place? How will new policies and programs be aligned with existing ones? What trends compete with the effort to engage all the employees in positive activities?

- **Inputs,** or resources or infrastructure: What raw materials will be used to conduct the effort for systemic change? Inputs can also include constraints on the system, such as regulations or funding gaps, which are barriers to your objectives.

- **Activities,** or interventions: How will resources for systemic change direct the course of change? Your intervention, and thus your logic model, should be guided by a clear risk analysis.

- **Outputs:** What evidence is there that the processes were performed as planned? Indicators might include the number of minorities, women, and people from the culture of difference hired and promoted, and the retention of these individuals.

- **Effects,** results, consequences, outcomes, or impacts: What kinds of changes come about as a direct or indirect result of the process of change?

Putting these elements together graphically gives the following basic structure for a logic model. The arrows between the boxes indicate that review and adjustment are an ongoing process—both in enacting the initiative and developing the model.

What Does a Logic Model Look Like?

There is no one right way to construct a logic model. There are many approaches, and a logic model can take on many forms. One possible approach follows, beginning with a generic logic model and an explanation of its components.

Plan to Evaluate and Learn From the Data

The primary purpose of this brief is to develop a logic model that helps you describe your own systematic diversity and inclusion process and identify outcomes and measures that will help you assess your cultural change and results. This step is offered briefly to make the point that the next step is to move forward with the evaluation in terms of putting plans in place to collect data on the measures you have identified and to use that data along with the logic model for learning. The figure on the next page identifies four additional elements toward that end, which can be added to the logic model.[15]

Data Sources and Methods: the sources for the data needed to track indicators and performance measures: Ask yourself how you will get the data that you need in the most efficient way now that you have identified my measures. If you used the criterion that data should already be available for the indicators you have chosen, then you should already know their data sources and how often they are available. However, you also need to determine how often to report that information and who will get it and how. Performance measures will likely require additional data collection that either you or your evaluator conducts. You can probably track some of that information, such as the measures of effort, on your own. However, you may need to use an external evaluator to collect data on the measures of effect (e.g., sources: standardized testing, state or local government databases; methods: surveys, focus groups, interviews).

Evaluation Questions: the questions you want to have answered by the data or decisions that you want to make based on your data: You should be able to make decisions based on your indicators and performance measures. Ask yourself: What strategic decisions can I make based on the

---

[15] (Ibid.)

information that will be generated? What consequences should be tied to achievement for good or bad performance? For example, are the indicators moving and if not, does that mean the components of the systemic change need to be modified?

What are the benefits and limitations of logic modeling?
You can probably envision a variety of ways in which you might use the logic model you have developed or how logic modeling can benefit your work. Here are a few advantages that experienced modelers have discovered:

• **Logic models integrate planning, implementation, and evaluation.** As a detailed description of your diversity strategy, from resources to results, the logic model is equally important for planning, implementing, and evaluating the systemic process of change. If you are a planner, the modeling process challenges you to think more like an evaluator. If your purpose is evaluation, the modeling prompts discussion of planning. And for those who implement, the modeling answers practical questions about how the work will be organized and managed.[16]

• **Logic models prevent mismatches between changes and efforts.** Planners often summarize an effort by listing its vision, mission, objectives, strategies, and action plans. Even with this information, it can be hard to tell how all the pieces fit together. By connecting changes and effects, a logic model helps avoid proposing systemic changes with no practical outcome, or anticipating outcomes with no supporting systemic changes. The ability to easily spot such mismatches is perhaps the main reason why so many logic models use a flow chart format.

• **Logic models leverage the power of partnerships.** As the W. K. Kellogg Foundation notes, refining a logic model is interactive or repeating process that allows participants to "make changes based on consensus-building and a logical process rather than on personalities, politics, or ideology. [17] The clarity of thinking that occurs from the process of building the model becomes an important part of the overall success of the systemic process." With a well-specified logic model, it is possible to note where the baton should be passed from one person or agency to another. This enhances collaboration and guards against things falling through the cracks.

---

[16] (Ibid.)
[17] (Kellogg Foundation 2004)

- **Logic models enhance accountability by keeping stakeholders focused on outcomes.** As Connie Schmitz and Beverly Parsons point out, a list of action steps usually function as a manager's guide for running a project by showing what staff or others need to do. In a coalition or collaborative partnership, the logic model makes it clear which effects each partner creates and how all those effects converge with a common goal. The family or nesting approach works well in a collaborative partnership because a model can be developed for each objective along a sequence of effects, thereby showing layers of contributions and points of intersection.

- **Logic models help planners to set priorities for allocating resources.** A comprehensive model will reveal where physical, financial, human, and other resources are needed. When planners are discussing options and setting priorities, a logic model can help them make resource-related decisions in light of how the program's activities and outcomes will be affected.

- **Logic models reveal data needs and provide a framework for interpreting results.** It is possible to design a documentation system that includes only beginning and end measurements. This is a risky strategy, with a good chance of yielding disappointing results. An alternative approach calls for tracking changes at each step along the planned sequence of effects. With a logic model, system planners can identify intermediate effects and define measurable indicators for them.

- **Logic models enhance learning by integrating research findings and practiced wisdom.** Most systemic changes are founded on assumptions about the behaviors and conditions that need to change and how they are subject to intervention. Frequently, there are different degrees of certainty about those assumptions. For example, some of the links in a logic model may have been tested and proved to be sound through previous research. Other linkages, by contrast, may never have been researched, tried, or thought of before. The explicit form of a logic model means that you can combine evidence-based practices from prior research with innovative ideas that veteran practitioners believe will make a difference. If you are armed with a logic model, it will be difficult for critics to claim that your work is not evidence-based.

- **Logic models define a shared language and shared vision for change.** The terms used in a model help to standardize the way people think and how they speak about change. It gets everyone rowing in the same direction and enhances communication with external audiences, such as the media or potential funders. Even stakeholders who are skeptical or antagonistic toward your work can be drawn into the discussion and development of a logic model. Once you've got them talking about the logical connections between systemic changes and effects, they are no longer criticizing from the sidelines. They become engaged in problem-solving, and they will do so in an open forum, where everyone can see their resistance to change or lack of logic, if that is the case.[18] Below is a sample of a logic model.

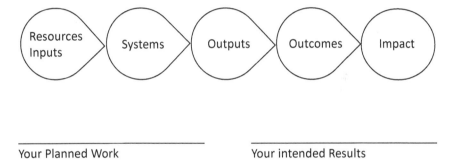

Your Planned Work   Your intended Results

Figure 3. The Basic Logic Model.

The most basic logic model is a picture of how you believe a particular structure within your system will work. It uses words and/or pictures to describe the sequence of processes that are predicted to bring about systemic changes and how these systemic changes are linked to those.

---

[18] (Kellog Foundation 2004)

Chapter 5

Inclusion Management Competencies for Systemic Approach to Change

Competencies of success are those that, when combined with knowledge, skills, abilities, and organizationally accepted behavior, create the codes of conduct that build and manage a culture of diversity and inclusion within the workplace. Thus, competencies may be considered talent-based interpretations of business needs. Based on this definition, competencies add value by communicating what people must know in order to help the business succeed.[19] This is imperative during competitive times. Challenged organizations commonly need to get attention for new solutions, because existing approaches, while comfortable, no longer add value.

In order to create an effective culture of inclusion at the workplace, employees must know what is expected of them. Competencies include the specific behaviors that enable performance in the workplace.[20] Employees need to know how organizational competencies affect their longevity and accountability within the company. Most employees view diversity and inclusion as a racial and ethnic concept by adhering to the old school ideas about civic diversity, when in fact organizational diversity competencies provide employees with an understanding of why managing diversity is part of their everyday tasks instead of why diversity is the right thing to do. The rest of this chapter will be about developing competencies for success and how to use them to manage diversity and inclusion at the orga-

---

[19] (Ledford 1995)
[20] (Ledford 1995a)

nizational level. Employees will understand through these competencies that everything they do at work relates to diversity and inclusion. These competencies will help them understand that diversity and inclusion are not abstract concepts without any tangible, consequential meaning. In fact, employees will see them as integrate components of their job performance.

There are four essential components that I recommend as part of the design of organizational competencies. They are inclusion management, customer service, team orientation, and adaptability.

Inclusion Management

Inclusion Management is closely linked to cultural competency, or the ability to work effectively across cultures by learning to communicate and work in a business setting with others. These competencies dictate the cultural climate of an organization regardless of employees' personal beliefs.[21]

This competency must provide a clear statement of what diversity and inclusion mean to an organization, and it must dictate what type of behavior is expected as a result from each employee. The definition of this standard must be clear and must include the different diverse group that must be represented within the workplace. It should be a statement that any employee can recognize, know, and understand when related to other competencies of success. For instance, this competency should address the following: diversity and inclusion at the organizational level are vehicles where all kinds and classes of people interact equitably; it signals collaboration with people of all races, nationalities, cultures, disabilities, ages, genders, and sexual orientations in an environment conducive to teamwork that will meet the company's bottom line.

Customer Service

It is essential to determine whether the competency should be defined in terms of trying to serve more the customer the same way as before or by finding a way to partner with the customer in a way that benefits both parties. What the customer and company roles are now and what they should be defines how change will be executed. This presents an opportunity to evaluate progress in terms of moving from the type of relationship that is judged to be unsatisfactory to a new type of relationship that will provide a shared advantage.[22] Customers must be defined as both internal and

---

[21] (Robinson 2000)
[22] (Collins 1994)

external customers; noting that the internal customers are employees and coworkers within the workplace.

Team Orientation

One aim of the communication competency is to articulate that people must get along with each other or work in teams. Team orientation means communicating the importance of transitioning from a situation where individuals are accountable to where people in teams share accountability. Team orientation implies shared fate among team members; it also implies accountability to a team leader or manager. The team in the context of this competency can be the entire organization or a business unit; a self-directed work team or a project team; or a quality improvement team. Team orientation is a state of mind as well as a behavioral practice. The advantage of this competency comes from presenting the concept in the organization's context and defining how diversity and inclusion will be gained.[23]

Adaptability

This refers the ability to change and apply behaviors and other competencies to different situations. The standard for adaptability must include compliance with new orders and directions or the ability to read situations and take personal responsibility for behaving accordingly. Adaptability is an active or passive competency. It is important to define the competency either in terms of the ability to follow orders in an acceptable manner or in terms of the "thinking person's" view of adaptability.[24] Each employee is able to work with others within the workplace and adapt to the everyday demands of the job to meet the company's bottom line.

The reason I recommend these competencies is because they all have a direct link to inclusion management. They affirm the behavioral understanding that everything an employee does at work relates to diversity and inclusion once they interact with another coworker.[25] Setting up these types of competencies to align them with inclusion management takes the guesswork out of what diversity and inclusion are and how they can be implemented in the workplace. For the very first time employees have a clear understanding of the expectation of inclusion within the workplace and how to implement them. There is a direct correlation to what they do at work and how to behave when working with others to meet the bottom line. Inclusion management does not make employees like each other; it

[23] (Hamel 1994)
[24] (Lawler 1995)
[25] (Robinson 2000)

teaches him/her how to work together in a diverse work environment to get the work done.

Note: There are companies that specialized in writing competencies that include diversity and inclusion standards for organizations. You may want to look up some of these companies before you embark in the development of them for your organization.

Chapter 6

Why Disproportionality Has a Great Impact in a Systemic Process of Change

As diversity continues to increase within the United States, one would tend to believe that racial disparity at the organizational level would also diminish, as would opportunities for minorities, women, people with disabilities, and people from the culture of difference would tend to increase as well. But the reality is that companies are not close to bridging the racial disparity gap[26] in corporate America. Many corporations must change the way they outreach, hire, promote, and retain diverse candidates. As we continue to move to a more globalized market, minorities have become the primary customers and investors in corporate America. I am writing this book because I believe that organizations at all levels have the responsibility and the power to create a culture of inclusion within their workforces and eliminate disparity gaps. One of the buzz words used in conjunction with diversity and inclusion right now is "equity." In order for us to speak about equity at work, we must first look at organizations making the structural changes necessary for it to occur. Disparities are a symptom of a lack of equity. In this chapter I address intentional purpose as one of most effective instruments to bridging the disparity gap at the organizational level.

---

[26] ("Persistent Racial Inequalities" 2011)

Disparities within the Workforce

Research done by the Russell Sage Foundation (RSF) shows that one of the most powerful ways to improve the lives and to distribute wealth among diverse populations is for them to be gainfully employed—with stable health benefits, opportunities to advance, opportunities for higher education, and the ability to save money for the future. The study tell us that "the Multi-City Study of Urban Inequality, RSF's largest single effort in the 1990s, was aimed at finding out why high rates of joblessness have persisted among minorities living in America's central cities. Despite a robust US economy, millions of low-skill, inner-city workers remain unemployed or stuck in low-paying, dead-end jobs. One explanation is that the economic restructuring of recent decades has increased the educational and skill requirements for most jobs and that most inner-city workers do not have the training and experience to qualify for these jobs. Many jobs, moreover, have moved from cities to the suburbs, stranding inner-city workers. The Sage Foundation's Multi-City Study found that these two factors, which researchers refer to as skill and spatial mismatches, tell only part of the story: persistent racial barriers, especially employer bias against hiring racial minorities, constitute an even more significant challenge to the job prospects of inner-city workers."[27]

This is careful social scientific research, and it contributes to a much better understanding of the mechanisms that produce and reproduce urban poverty and persistent racial gaps. These mechanisms are both structural and ideational; the processes that lead to discrimination in employment, for example, includes both structural factors, like urban transportation, and ideational factors, such as racial stereotyping by recruiters, hiring managers, and individuals involved in the hiring process.[28]

Diverse External Customer Base

Leah Smiley, founder and president of the Society for Diversity, explains how in today's economic environment, global expansion is a business imperative. The Internet and technology make this feat easier, but there are some things that organizations must know about culturally diverse audiences in order to be successful in acquiring a larger share of the global market.

For one, diversity, inclusion, and multi-cultural competence are not the same terms as affirmative action or quotas. In the past, some groups

---

[27] (Russell Sage Foundation 1990)
[28] (Ibid.)

implemented affirmative action requirements as if they were in a fire sale by hiring and promoting diverse individuals regardless their abilities to perform the work. Their intentions were good, but the methods were bad. This caused a lot resentment among the seasoned employees, and sat up the new hires or promoted employees for failure. Fast forward fifty years, and businesses recognize the value that diversity and inclusion brings to the table, particularly as it pertains to building market share and improving competitive, global positioning.

Here are a few related facts:

- The World Bank estimates that the global middle class is likely to grow from 430 million in 2000 to 1.2 billion in 2030. China and India will account for two-thirds of the expansion.

- According to the US Census Bureau, the number of business start-ups (brick and mortar and others) by minorities and women outpaces start-ups by the majority population.

- According to a recent study by Socio-Economic Trends, in heterosexual households, females make 43 percent of the financial decisions versus 31 percent of joint decisions.

- The Latino population is growing rapidly due to births and immigration." For those reasons, the Pew Hispanic Center projections indicate that Latinos "will account for three quarters of the growth in the nation's labor force from 2010 to 2020; Latinos buying power is worth one trillion dollars now in the United States, according to a new Nielsen report.

- According the US Census Bureau, one in five Americans is considered disabled, and the number of disabled Americans will increase with the aging population.

- The lesbian, gay, bisexual, and transgender community's buying power is fast approaching $800 billion this year, according to research by Witeck-Combs Communications and Marketresearch.com. A recent study by Witeck-Combs and Harris Interactive also found a substantial majority (70 percent) of gay men and lesbians report that they have switched products or service providers because they found out the company had engaged in actions that are perceived as harmful to the LGBTQ community.

In this way, affirmative action is different from diversity. Affirmative action had nothing to do with customers, and it is a policy that only affects organizations operating in the United States. If we honestly look at the policy as a whole, it did achieve its purpose of including underrepresented groups in the workplace. And, those groups (women and minorities) do work hard to contribute to the bottom line. But diversity has everything to do with competitive advantage and customers—including new markets, global business opportunities, and new organizational strategies. It is the future of economic viability and sustainability.

Consider who your clients were ten to twenty years ago. This historic reference is necessary to reflect on who your customers were, how their needs have changed, and how you can anticipate their future wants.

Not only do companies need to know specifically who is currently purchasing their services but how projected demographic and economic changes will affect future business. They also need to figure out how they can tap into additional, or new, revenue streams.[29]

Intentional Purpose one of the Tools to Bridging the Gap

Strategy I. Intentional Purpose
Intentional purpose means planned strategies designed by the leadership team of an organization to create a tangible impact in increasing the numbers on internal and/or external diverse customers. These strategies are put in place to create a culture of inclusion at the organizational level.

The inclusion revolution framework incorporates intentional purpose (IP) as one of those strategies necessary to impact tangible cultural change within the workplace. The key element of IP effectiveness is communication. For IP to have success in addressing disproportionality within the workforce, every employee in the organization must have a complete understanding of it. IP is not a hidden strategy; it is a component of the culture of change. As employees go through professional development to learn about the strategic plan on diversity and inclusion, they also need to know what the goals of the organization are to hire and promote diverse candidates. Employees also need to understand the reasons behind these efforts and their impact on retention of the new hires.

Companies that manage change effectively are more likely to have a formal, systematic process and a dedicated staff that includes internal and

---

[29] (Smiley, 2013)

external communicators compared to organizations that manage change less well, according to research by Towers Watson.

According to the study, leadership activities, which include executive sponsorship for organizational change, developing a clear vision of desired organizational change, creating an integrated communication and change management strategy, and creating strong employee motivation for making organizational change have the most influence in the overall success of an organization's change.

Effective communication is an important element of change management and, if both are done well, can significantly impact financial performance. Companies highly effective at both communication and other change management activities are 2.5 times as likely to outperform companies that have not.

"Organizational change is a continuous reality. Regardless of the type of change an organization experiences or where it is located, the critical change activities remain constant. Organizations that get the leading, measuring and sustaining activities right will be the ones that experience the greatest success." The 2011–2012 Towers Watson Change and Communication ROI Study includes responses from 604 organizations in various industries from around the world.[30]

Strategy II. Workforce Population Index or Visible Diversity
As a systemic process of change is put in place at the organizational level, companies must keep in mind that once intentional purpose is established for the hiring and promoting of a diverse population, the number must be significant enough to create a tangible impact. Most companies use their community of service population index to set their recruitment goals, but in most cases, this approach does not create the visible diversity needed to be an organization of excellence.[31] Visible diversity must be composed of a third of the total workforce population. This means equal job distribution that includes upper management positions as well as entry level ones.

The workforce population index is one of the best tools to determine what percentage of a diverse representation an organization should have.

---

[30] (Watson, 2011–2012)
[31] (Robinson M., 2000)

Income Gap

In 2010, the latest year for which data are available, white women earned 78.1 percent compared to white men, African American women earned 89.8 percent compared to African American men, Hispanic women earned 91.3 percent compared to Hispanic men, and Asian women earned 79.7 percent compared to Asian men. The wage gap is lower for black and Hispanic women in part because wages for people of color tend to be lower overall. This gap occurs within racial and ethnic groups as well. In 2010, according to the Census Bureau, African Americans earned only 58.7 percent of what whites earned, while Hispanics earned only 69.1 percent of what whites earned. The American Association of University Women tackled the pay gap question by looking at workers of the same educational background—the same kind of college and the same grades, holding the same kinds of jobs, and having made the same choices about marriage and number of kids. They found that college-educated women earn 5 percent less the first year out of school than their male peers. Ten years later, even if they keep working on par with those men, the women earn 12 percent less.

As we look at the data reflecting disparities within the workforce, a systemic process of change through my framework helps organizations be more in tune with the steps they must follow to be intentional and succeed in creating a culture of inclusion.

Chapter 7

The Generational Impact on a Systemic Process of Change

This is the first time in the history of the United States that we have four generations working together side by side. (There is the fifth generation brewing in the workforce. It is the general Z or net. I will only address the first four.) They are the mature or traditionalists, the baby boomers, the generation X or Xers, and generation Y or the millennials. According to Lee Hecht Harrison, 60 percent of employers are experiencing tension between employees of different generations.[32] This chapter will help you have a look at each generation for a better understanding of their behaviors and attitudes as you pursue the implementation of a culture of inclusion in your organization. Different generations within the workplace are creating such cultural impact that as part of a systemic change, we cannot overlook their influence.

Let's start by defining a generation. It is a group of individuals born in approximately the same time period who generally share similar behaviors and attitudes, and, I would add, use technology in similar ways. I added technology because it has created a new way of thinking, behaving, and acting for the Xers and millennials.

Chronologically they were born in the following order:

- mature/traditionalists (born 1922–1945)

---

[32] (Hecht 1994)

- baby boomers (born 1946–1964)

- generation X (born 1965–1982)

- millennials/generation Y (born 1983–1997)

Why is it important to understand the different generations within the workplace? Because it provides

- more effective communication/fewer misunderstandings;

- increased recruitment and employee retention;

- more effective motivational methods;

- better-formed expectations; and

- increased productivity and teamwork.

These are the generational characteristics that looking at the research I found. You may also see that there are some a crossover characteristics between generations depending on how the individual was raised. Also this information is not to say the every one born during the years given is exactly as described. There are many exceptions to the rule. I have also found that there are some discrepancies in the block of years in which a generation spans give or take two to three years.

- **Mature or Traditionalist Generation (1922–1945)**

- **Type: Adaptive**

Characteristics:
- value hard work and thriftiness

- emphasize traditional morals

- hold work values of conformity, consistency, and uniformity

- value safety and security

- value loyalty and commitment

- value the system over individual enterprise

Learner Characteristics:
- respect authority of educator

- find technology challenging

Baby Boomer Generation (1946–1964)
Type: Idealist

Characteristics:
- have the buy now, pay later mentality

- are rebellious and question the status quo

- have moved away from extended families

- identify with their jobs

- equate work with self-worth

- are driven and dedicated

- believe they can change the world

- believe they do not have to grow old and sedentary

Learner Characteristics:
- accustomed to being dependent on educator

- want to have a say in own learning

- want a caring environment

- respond to positive feedback, desire to do well

- connect learning to outcomes

- want to feel connected to others in the learning environment

Generation X (1965–1982)
Type: Reactive

Characteristics:
- are ironic, cynical, adept, clever, and resourceful

- define themselves in opposition to their parents

- do not belong to any group

- know how to win

- manage independently and participate in discussions

- balance job and leisure time

- adapt well to change

- are tolerant of alternative lifestyles

- become anxious when faced with the many decisions of adulthood

- believe that early adulthood is the time where they must determine the meaning in their lives

- try to attain several goals all at once

Learner Characteristics:
- are comfortable with technology

- are self-directed learners; work in teams

- want clear information of practical value

- use fun and humor; games and activities are appropriate

- can manage delayed gratification

Generation Y, Millennials (1983–1997)
Type: Civic

Characteristics:
- are optimistic, assertive, positive, and friendly; they believe they will be rich

- accept authority; are rule followers

- are accustomed to structure

- are cooperative team players, gravitating toward group activities

- are the most racially and ethnically diverse generation

- think of themselves as global

Learner Characteristics:
- grew up experiencing digital media and internet access

- use mobile devices to access and process information

- technology is expected to be available to them

- prefer to work in groups and teams

- have an "always on" connectivity that blurs work time and learning

- want "augmented reality"—real work environments similar to the work setting such as simulations and virtual reality

- are active learners; seek innovations; want immediate response to learning needs and questions

- have difficulty focusing on one thing; prefer to multitask

- have difficulty honing skills of critical analysis necessary to read between the lines due to volume of available information

- use "hyper-learning" models as opposed to linear acquisition of information; want to construct information on their own; are independent

- enjoy being mentored by older generations

The generation Xers and millennials are the most multicultural diverse, open, and accepting generations of our times. These two generations are looking at the mature and the baby boomer generations and wondering why they are still talking about race, ethnicity, color, and LGBTQ. These two generations made it possible for a black candidate to be elected president in the United States for the first time in the history of the country. They started the campaign for gay rights by asking openly gay personalities in all media to share their message. They also are fighting hard for the awareness and importance of rights for same-sex couples, as well as other human rights around the world. They have the most multiracial unions in society because they feel very comfortable choosing whomever they want to be with without worrying about what others would say. The Xers are the first generation that thought that they had to have fun at work on a regular basis, and became very aware of the separation between family and work. For them family is first, and work is secondary. The millennial generation, on the other hand, is by far the most analyzed, most marketed to, and most intriguing generation to date. It is a generation comprised of individuals who are extremely ambitious and not only have high expectations for themselves, but also for those around them, including their friends, families, communities, and businesses. It is also a generation that has been shaped by tragic world events such as 9/11 and natural disasters such as Hurricane Katrina. The result is a group that has developed a strong social conscience, which is amplified by technology.

Observation
According to research the Xers and millennials are a generation of young people accustomed to options. They are acutely aware of their marketing power and influence. They demand customization and instantaneous feedback. And their demands are usually answered.[33] These two generations like to feel welcome at work. They will not stay if they feel that they are not accepted. Millennials will have at least seven different careers in their lifetimes. They are poised to pursue career paths different from prior generations as they enter the workforce. In order to succeed, millennials believe they need to pursue higher education, obtain transferable skills, and hold a variety of different jobs or perhaps even multiple career paths. They believe success equals a career where they do meaningful and personally fulfilling work that has a positive impact on others, while earning a high salary.

Hiring managers and supervisors recognize some of the plans and ambitions of millennials, but they still hold misconceptions by clinging to

---

[33] (GreenBook the guide for marketing)

stereotypes of the millennial generation. The millennials anticipate that the younger generation will have different work experiences when compared to older generations—most notably by holding more jobs and having more flexibility in location and hours worked.[34] One of the most pervasive misconceptions among managers and supervisors is that the chance to earn a high salary, perhaps without putting in the appropriate amount of effort and time, is the primary motivating factor for young workers. Managers also place more emphasis on the role of obtaining transferable skills and setting career goals with managers to give millennials the chance to seek opportunities to advance their careers.[35]

Many boomers plan to continue working past traditional retirement age, and many will remain in positions of leadership. The things important to millennials and generation Xers, and increasingly to boomers as well—like work-life balance, flexible scheduling, rewards for results, and options to work from home—will become more integral parts of workplace culture[36].

The importance of studying the different generations is to realize that diversity and inclusion takes into account people working together to continue to stay employed, to address the diversity strategic plan, and to achieve the organizational goals.

---

[34] (Kersten, 2002.)
[35] (Board, January 28, 2011)
[36] (Staying Ahead of the Curve 2003)

Chapter 8

The Impact of Unconscious Bias in a Systemic Process of Change

This chapter deals with unconscious biases and the impact those biases have when dealing and working with diverse populations. Every time I bring up unconscious biases when I am working with employers or employees I find that several people will swear that they don't have any biases. The truth of the matter is that all of us have biases about something or someone at some point in our lives. Sometimes the unconscious biases are so deep seated in our consciousness that we define the behavior as part of a personality trait. The word *unconscious*, when based in organizational diversity, means that a person may not be aware of his or her behavior when interacting with another person; in some instances it takes someone else to point out the behavior to make the person aware of his or her impact on others. The other definition of unconscious bias is a social behavior driven by learned stereotypes that operate automatically, and therefore unconsciously, when one interacts with other people. It is an automatic decision-making response. According to the research, when we see something or someone that does not fit into our everyday paradigm, we launch into an automatic decision-making response before we even think.

Unconscious biases within the workplace can produce unequal opportunities and outcomes for employees depending on their diversity. Researchers have found out also that unconscious bias, hidden bias, or implicit bias arose as a way to explain why discrimination persists, even though polling and other research clearly shows that people oppose it. Initially, some researchers conjectured that people sought to hide their bias from pollsters and simply lied about their views for fear of appearing prejudiced.

However, in 1995, Doctors Anthony Greenwald and Mahzarin R. Banaji theorized that it was possible that our social behavior was not completely under our conscious control. In *Implicit Social Cognition: Attitudes, Self-Esteem and Stereotypes*, Greenwald and Banaji argue that much of our social behavior is driven by learned stereotypes that operate automatically—and therefore unconsciously—when we interact with other people. Three years later, Greenwald et al. developed the Implicit Association Test (IAT), which has become the standard bearer for measuring implicit bias.[37] (I will provide information later how to access IAT for your own assessment of biases.)

Unconscious biases can decrease if a systemic process of change is put in place, such as organizational diversity. Studies have shown that diverse social environments (at workplaces, colleges, etc.) can help lower implicit bias among its workers.[38] As a result of intentional purpose, organization-wide understanding of the strategic plan on inclusion management, and exposure to positive exemplars, employees learn to model the behavior of success expected from all of them and set forth by the leadership of the organization to create a culture of inclusion.

The inclusion revolution framework is so effective in creating a culture of inclusion because it helps employees be aware of how and why unconscious biases may cause disruptions at work, and by acknowledging those unwritten rules or behaviors, an employee may salvage or modify his or her interactive behavior with other coworkers, supervisors, etc. These behaviors are sometimes so small that only people affected by them are aware of them. These settled behaviors are sometimes detrimental to the retention of a diverse population within the workplace, and for that reason they are called "micro." These micro behaviors can be positive or negative. Diverse populations are exposed to them on a daily basis and have learned to live, cope, and survive with them. They can be micro affirmations or micro inequalities. Research shows that these types of micro behaviors are the major reason why diverse populations either stay in a job and work hard to achieve the American dream or give up and seek employment elsewhere. Diverse populations that don't feel welcome at work start looking for a new job within the first thirty days of employment.[39]

---

[37] (Banaji 1991)
[38] (Brown 2005)
[39] (Gilgoff 2009)

Micro affirmations versus Micro inequalities

Micro affirmations and micro inequalities are small acts that are often ephemeral and hard to notice; they are public and private behaviors that are often unconscious but very effective, and they occur whenever people wish to help others to succeed or make them fail.

Micro affirmations

They are tiny acts of opening doors, gestures of inclusion and caring, and graceful acts of listening. Micro affirmations lie in the practice of generosity, in consistently giving credit to others, and in providing comfort and support when others are in distress, whether there has been a failure at the bench, an idea that did not work out, or a public attack. Micro affirmations include the myriad details of fair, specific, timely, consistent, and clear feedback that help a person build on strength and correct weakness.[40]

What are micro inequalities?

They are defined as "apparently small events which are often ephemeral and hard-to-prove, events which are covert, often supposedly unintentional, frequently unrecognized by others not targeted." micro inequalities have been primary scaffolding for discrimination in the United States. Micro inequalities are a serious problem since much of this bias is unconscious and unrecognized—and even hard to believe when described—unless videotaped.[41]

They are those subliminal behaviors that impede diverse employee success or advancement within the organization. Such behaviors include "little" issues such as acts of disrespect, failures in performance feedback, mistakenly leaving someone off a list, not introducing someone at meetings or events (or mistakenly introducing a person as someone else of the same race), intentionally not providing all the information needed to complete a task, omitting the person from meetings and office parties, spreading rumors about employee competency levels, not speaking to the employee, or acting indifferent toward him or her. Micro inequalities also include someone talking to the diverse employee as if he or she has never worked with someone diverse before and acting scared around the diverse employee. If direct supervisors give the diverse employees unreasonable goals to achieve, set up higher expectations than the other employees, pass them up for promotions for less-qualified, non-diverse employees,

---

[40] (Rowe 2008)
[41] (Ibid.)

micro inequalities are at play. The Korn/Ferry International recruiting world-class leadership talent company in its report about employee retention found that 34 percent of those who left jobs because of diversity-related issues said they probably would have stayed if managers had recognized their abilities and talents.[42]

There is an extremely close correlation between micro inequalities, unconscious biases, and managing a diverse workforce; unconscious biases continue to be the major barrier to bridging the disparity gap within the workforce.

Mary Rowe in her research points out that by helping managers, supervisors, and employees to be aware of micro affirmations and micro inequalities within the workplace, organizations can become healthier in managing diversity in a diverse workforce. This awareness may help an organization in the recruitment, retention, and promotion of diverse populations.

Many micro inequalities are not conscious, but affirming others can become a conscious as well as unconscious practice that prevents other unconscious slights. [43]

Unconscious behavior can be modified if supervisors are aware of what is going on with their employees. There are "small things" that tend to go unnoticed and not followed up on because the misperception that they are small or insignificant, when in fact negative behaviors are contagious, dangerous, and detrimental to the efforts to create diversity and inclusion within the workplace.

Habitual Acceptance

It is a micro inequality behavior that an employee displays, often at work, and it becomes acceptable behavior by the people around him or her. What you will hear when someone points out the behavior is "that is the way so and so is." Managers and supervisors also become immune to habitual acceptance behavior and end up making excuses for those employees instead of making sure that the negative behavior is addressed, and the employee is counseled, or written up until that behavior is modified. An example of habitual acceptance is the employee that refuses to work or complains when he or she works with someone he or she perceives as "different." So instead of counseling the employee, the supervisor or manager does not put him or her in a crew or a project with someone that the

---

[42] (The Art of Science of Talent 2008)
[43] (Rowe 2008)

employee dislikes. This is a minute example of habitual acceptance at the organizational level. Another example is sexual harassment and human abuse.

What should be done?

- Managers and supervisors can and should pay attention to the "small things."

- The principles of appreciative inquiry are relevant to micro affirmations: leading rather than pushing; building on strength and success, rather than first identifying faults and weaknesses.

- Small things are especially important with respect to feelings. (Managers must be impartial about facts, but it is often appropriate and helpful to affirm people's feelings.) As it happens, it is relatively easy for most people to practice and teach how to affirm feelings. This is important because the mechanics" of affirmation are not trivial in human affairs; attitudes may follow behavior just as behavior may follow attitudes.

- Whenever a question is brought to us about how to change offensive behavior—whether our own behavior or that of another—we can teach the principles of changing behavior, and we can explore options about how to do it.[44]

Where diversity is concerned, unconscious bias creates hundreds of seemingly irrational circumstances every day in which people make choices that seem to make no sense and be driven only by overt prejudice, even when they are not. Of course, there are still some cases where people are consciously hateful, hurtful, and biased. These behaviors need to be watched, addressed, and most importantly not ignored even if there are small. But it is also important to recognize that the concept of unconscious bias does not only apply to "them." It applies to all of us. Each one of us has some groups with which we consciously feel uncomfortable, even as we castigate others for feeling uncomfortable with our own groups. These conscious patterns of discrimination are problematic, but, again, they pale in comparison to the unconscious patterns that impact us every day. Unconscious perceptions govern many of the most important decisions we make and have a profound effect on the lives of many people in many ways. The inclusion revolution framework provides the platform to truly integrate the

---

[44] (Rowe, 2008)

awareness of unconscious biases among the employees, and works with them by bringing this important and so often dismissed behavior to light.

Testing Your Unconscious Bias Index

I was introduced to the Implicit Association Test (IAT) by one of my colleagues soon after it was created. It is the most effective tool available for testing one's own unconscious bias. The IAT was created more than ten years ago by a consortium of researchers from Harvard University, the University of Virginia, and the University of Washington. It has now been used by millions of people in over twenty countries. Researchers have used the test to study many aspects of organizational and social performance, ranging from hiring and recruitment to promotion practices. To take the IAT, without charge, go to https://implicit.harvard.edu/impl. I always recommend the leadership team, supervisors, and managers take the IAT to help them understand how their own biases rank.

The Organizational Unconscious

Unconscious behavior is not just individual; it influences organizational culture as well. This explains why so often our best attempts at creating corporate cultural change with diversity efforts seems to fall frustratingly short—to not deliver on the intended promises. Organizational culture is more or less an enduring collection of basic assumptions and ways of interpreting what a given organization has invented, discovered, or developed in learning to cope with its internal and external influences. Unconscious organizational patterns, or "norms" of behavior, exert an enormous influence over organizational decisions, choices, and behaviors. These deepseated company characteristics often are the reason that our efforts to change organizational behavior fail. Despite our best conscious efforts, the organizational unconscious perpetuates the status quo and keeps old patterns, values, and behavioral norms firmly rooted.[45] The inclusion revolution framework systemic process of change makes employees aware of unconscious biases in the workplace and how they affect the retention of diverse population. It brings out the elephant in the room by having a frank dialogue about how to deal with biases that some people may not be aware of at the individual or organizational levels.

The Level Playing Field Institute is committed to eliminating barriers faced by underrepresented people of color in science. It is a San Francisco-based nonprofit that studies, identifies, and removes hidden biases from

---

[45] (Judge 2004)

the classroom to the board room, and has designated ten steps each employee can take to mitigate hidden bias.

Top Ten Ways to Combat Hidden Bias

1. Recognize that as human beings, our brains make mistakes without us even knowing it. The new science of "unconscious bias" applies to how we perceive other people. We're all biased and becoming aware of our own biases will help us mitigate them in the workplace.

2. Reframe the conversation to focus on fair treatment and mutual respect, and away from discrimination and "protected classes." Review every aspect of the employment life cycle for hidden bias—screening resumes, interviews, onboarding, assignment process, mentoring programs, performance evaluation, identifying high performers, promotion, and termination.

3. Ensure that anonymous employee surveys are conducted companywide to first understand what specific issues of hidden bias and unfairness might exist at your workplace. Each department or location may have different issues.

4. Conduct anonymous surveys with former employees to understand what were the issues they faced, what steps could be taken for them to consider coming back, whether they encourage or discourage prospective employees from applying for positions at your company and whether they encourage or discourage prospective customers and clients from using your company's products or services.

5. Offer customized training based upon survey results of current and former employees that includes examples of hidden bias, forms of unfairness that are hurtful and demotivating, and positive methods to discuss these issues.

6. Offer an anonymous, third-party, complaint channel such as an ombudsperson; since most of the behaviors that employees perceive as unfair are not covered by current laws, e.g. bullying, very subtle bias. Existing formal complaint channels simply don't work.

7. Initiate a resume study within your industry, company, and/or department to see whether resumes with roughly equivalent

education and experience are weighted equally, when the names are obviously gender, racially, or culturally distinct.

8. Launch a resume study (If you are doing your own diverse recruitment) within your company and/or department to reassign points based on earned accomplishments versus accidents of birth, e.g. take points off for someone who had an unpaid internship, and add points for someone who put him or herself through college.

9. Support projects that encourage positive images of persons of color, people with disabilities, LGBTQ people, and women. Distribute stories and pictures widely that portray stereotype-busting images—posters, newsletters, annual reports, speaker series, podcasts. Many studies show that the mere positive image of specific groups of people can combat our hidden bias.

10. Identify, support, and collaborate with effective programs that increase diversity in the pipeline. Reward employees who volunteer with these groups, create internships and other bridges, and celebrate the stories of those who successfully overcome obstacles.[46]

Many companies also choose to undergo an organizational diversity audit. Most organizational audits assess the conscious layers of organizational behavior. What do people think, believe, and see about what's going on in the organization.[47]

---

[46] (Proven Strategies for Addressing Unconscious Bias in the Workplace 2008)
[47] (Ibíd.)

Chapter 9

Diversity and Inclusion Readiness Assessment Tool

The diversity and inclusion readiness assessment is a tool that I created for my framework to help organizations determine where they are in terms of diversity and inclusion progress. You may see that your organization may have some of the combination of the different levels of readiness that I will describe in this section of the book, and you will also see how to achieve a true level of diversity and inclusion excellence at the organizational level.

I have developed four types of organizations to illustrate levels of diversity and inclusion readiness. There are the struggling or survival-driven organizations, the status quo or maintenance-driven organizations, the solid or mission-driven organizations, and the progressive or excellence-driven organizations. I have also developed nine indicators to illustrate progress and impact: workforce composition; diversity standards (policy, funding, and evaluation process): diverse workforce in leadership roles; leadership professional development for a diverse workforce; internal leadership support; diverse supplier vendor component; finances; leadership accountability on diversity and inclusion; and disproportionality index/analysis, i.e. workforce capital vendor supplier.

The Struggling or Survival-Driven Organizations
The struggling or survival-driven organizations have very little diversified workforce composition. They tell the world that they believe in diversity, but no efforts are made to implement an inclusive environment. In most cases they don't have a strategic plan or policies to reflect any commitment

to diversity. There is no funding allocated for a diversity position, nor an evaluation process to determine how diversity is implemented or measured. The leadership team is mostly composed of non-minority males that are very resistant to incorporating diversity as a valuable resource in business. Recruitment, retention, and promotion of diverse populations is non-existent. This type of organization is very comfortable believing that having non-minority women in the organization is enough to show diversity, however none of these women are in top management positions nor will they ever be. The vendor supplier component is non-existent, and there is no desire to build one. This type of organization has a loss and negative bottom line. There are no accountability standards in place to measure failures or successes.

The Status Quo or Maintenance-Driven Organization

This type of organization starts thinking that having a diverse workforce is a valuable component of business practices, so the beginnings of the intent to hire diverse employees starts to emerge. A diversity plan is thought of, but diversity is not yet part of the strategic planning of the organization. Diversity is implemented as a professional development component for the staff, but the attempt to make employees aware of diversity is through civic diversity practices, and diversity program or initiatives are used to convey the feeling of diversity within the organization. An individual within the organization is asked to lead diversity efforts as another job duty and responsibility. This person in many cases does not have the expertise or the support of the leadership team to have an impact on policy or change. The leadership team starts learning the importance of diversity within the workplace, but the top management has no commitment to diversity, and some of them are still questioning the need for diversity in the first place. Champions of the cause are few. Vendor supplier diversity is non-existent, and there are no plans to build one. Diverse suppliers emerge only by accident. A diverse population is hired only for entry level positions, but there are none in management positions. Financial stability starts to emerge. There are no accountability standards in place to measure failures or successes.

Solid or Mission-Driven Organizations

This type of organization is somewhat diverse but struggles with the retention of minorities. In most cases there are quotas for minority recruitment to meet quotas or regulations. A person is hired to lead diversity efforts, and money is allocated to support this position. The person in this position is not considered part of the management team, which limits his or her power and influence within the organization. Diversity efforts become one of the items in the strategic plan or the organization. There are very few diverse employees in upper management positions, and the few that make it are under constant scrutiny for their performance. Grooming and mentoring of diverse employees start to emerge, and these actions are intentionally driven. Retention of diverse employees becomes a concern for the administration. The leadership team buys into the belief that diversity is a must within the workplace. Some members of upper management are still stuck in civic diversity mode, impeding the progress of a systemic process of change. A diverse vendor supplier base emerges, but spending goals are not in place. The organization is financially strong, and the beginning of a systemic process of inclusion for change starts to take over. No accountability standards to measure failures or successes are in place.

Progressive or Excellence-Driven Organizations

These types of organizations have visible diversity within different levels of the organization. They use organizational population indexes for hiring and promoting. All diversity efforts are based on the organizational strategic plan and its competencies of success. Professional development on inclusion management is known and practiced by all the employees within the organization. The organization goes beyond hiring a person to lead the diversity effort, but also allocates a line item in the budget to pay and sustain this position. The person hired is part of the upper management team and has great power and influence within the organization. Upper management is now expected to groom and mentor several diverse employees at a time. Support from upper management, the board of directors, and the trustees is visible and expected. Leadership is unified. Supplier diversity goals are put in place, and centralized purchasing is practiced. A person is hired to coordinate procurement efforts. This person is an expert in minority business and women owned enterprises, small business outreach and development. Yearly salary is determined according to vendor outreach and internal vendor match success. First tier vendors are required to have a diverse vendor portfolio. The organization is strong and above the bottom line. Measurable accountability outcomes are put place to measure failures and successes. Performance appraisals have diversity standards that include recruitment and retention expectations for all the employees.

The diversity and inclusion readiness assessment is a great tool to define where your organization is in terms of creating a systemic process of change.

Indicators

Workforce composition: This refers to the diverse populations present within the workforce of an organization. This indicator helps organizations realize that their workforce must mimic the communities they serve.

Diversity indicators: This refers to policies and funding appropriated to pay for the person or persons in charge of running the diversity efforts for the organization, and evaluation processes put in place to track failures and successes.

Diverse workforce in leadership roles: This indicator is extremely important to an organization that is truly committed to diversity and inclusion. The impact of a diverse workforce in leadership roles tells employees that these individuals are part of the organization's power and influence, which is a powerful message for recruitment and retention of a diverse workforce.

Leadership development for a diverse workforce: This refers to how management grooms and mentors diverse employees by providing the tools and skills necessary to advance within the organization. Organizations that are excellence driven require that management always grooms and mentors diverse employees throughout the organization at all times.

Internal leadership support refers to the commitment of the management team to support and establish a solid organization, which knows that diversity and inclusion is another great practice of doing business in a global economy.

Diverse supplier vendor indicator: This refers to the ability to create a diverse vendor base, which the organization can use to promote diversity and inclusion. This also means that the organization has established concrete spending goals and is actively seeking a diverse vendor for company's projects.

Finances: This indicator refers to the stability of the company and how the financial success of the company goes hand-in-hand with creating a culture of inclusion.

NOTE: Something you need to be aware of even if an organization has a strong and positive financial bottom line; the organization will never move to excellence until a systemic process for inclusion and diversity is in place. It is only when diversity and inclusion are in place that an organization moves to a competitive position within the global market; diverse populations are part of sharing the wealth of success within the workplace.

Leadership accountability: This indicator refers to the standards put in place to measure the success of diversity and inclusion practice by every employee within the organization and how the leadership team takes ownership of the success of inclusion. See chapter 13 on accountability for performance appraisal recommendations.

Disproportionality Indexes: This indicator refers to the ability to collect, analyze, and share data for continuing improvement. Part of this data collection includes the recruitment, retention, grooming, mentoring, and promotion of a diverse workforce.

Progressive or excellence-driven organizations are in a constant state of improvement and reevaluation. They make sure that all their employees are aware and practice a culture of inclusion. The leadership support and commitment is visible; diversity and inclusion results are tangible; the organizational bottom line is met; and a culture of inclusion is practiced at every level of the organization by each employee.

The table that follows offers a visual understanding of all the levels of diversity readiness of organizations. It will help you determine where your company is and how ready it is to move toward becoming excellence driven.

This table is one of the first tools that an organization should look at in determining its level of diversity readiness

Different Levels of Diversity and Inclusion Readiness					
Indicators	TYPE OF ORGANIZATIONS				Excellence Index
	Struggling Org. Survival Driven	Status Quo Org. Maintenance Driven	Solid Org. Mission Driven	Progressive Org. *Excellence Driven	Constant Improvement Reevaluation Process
Workforce Composition	Not diversified at all	A minority recruitment intent is put in place	Somewhat diverse but struggles with retention of minorities. Hires minorities to meet quotas or regulations	Diversified and Globalized. Hires skillful, talented individuals. Uses organizational population indexes for hiring and promoting	A C U
Diversity Indicators ◊ Policy ◊ Funding ◊ Evaluation Process	None None None	◊ A Diversity Plan is thought of ◊ Diversity Policy emerges ◊ Civic Diversity guides the "program"	Only a few diverse employees in upper management positions including women	All diversity indicators in place Inclusion is seen as a systemic process shared by all Line item in the organizational budget	L T U R E
Diverse Workforce In leadership roles	None	An employee is asked to coordinate "Diversity Program"	A person is hired to lead diversity efforts. Just a few diverse employees in upper management	Goes beyond hiring diverse candidates and also compensates them accordingly	O F
Leadership professional development for a Diverse Workforce	None	Starts to emerge, but no funding is allocated	Grooming & mentoring of women, minorities, employees with disabilities, and other people from cultures of difference emerges, but action is not intentional	Upper management is now expected & required to groom and mentor several diverse employees at a time	I N C
Internal Leadership Support	None	Very passive, questioning the need for diversity by some	Buy in by the leadership. Some of the leadership still stuck on civic diversity.	Upper management and board of directors support is visible and expected. Leadership is unified	L U S I
Diverse Supplier Vendor component	None	None	A department emerges. No participation goals are in place.	Internal participation goals are in place First-tier vendors are required to have a diverse vendor portfolio.	O N
Finances	Loss and negative bottom line	Financial stability starts to emerge	Financially strong	Strong and above bottom line	I S
Leadership Accountability on Diversity & Inclusion	None	None	A systemic process to inclusion starts to emerge	Measureable outcomes are put in place. Success is also measured as part of job performance.	P R
Disproportionality Index/Analysis Workforce Capital Vendor Supplier	None	None	Retention and promotion of women, minorities, people with disabilities and people from the culture of difference is a must. Intentional vendor supplier relationships are established now. A person is hired to coordinate procurement efforts. This person is an expert in MBE/WBE/Small business outreach & development. Yearly salary is determined according to vendor outreach and internally vendor matched success		E S E N T

Chapter 10

The Power of Diverse Groups in a Systemic Process of Change

I was born in a little town surrounded by the Andes Mountain in Venezuela. My biological father was the first person of color who ever lived in my little town at that time. He suffered a lot of discrimination and hardship but never allowed our family to experience that suffering. My oldest sister, Elva, was accused of screaming in the school intercom one day even though she was not even in the same area when the incident occurred. She was severely punished and beaten by the teacher. The injuries were so severe that she was not able to walk for a few days after the beating. My sister was the only child of color in a school of one hundred students. The minute my father heard about the incident, he launched an investigation and hired an attorney. People in the community were shocked that my father took such action—action that in the 1950s was unheard of. The investigation revealed that my sister was not the child who screamed in the loud speaker, nor was she on the premises at the time. My father won the case against the school, and a financial settlement was reached between my father and the school before the case went to trial. My father, instead of taking the money, made an agreement with the school. His first request was that the teacher who hurt my sister was fired right away—she was; the second demand was that no child would ever be punished physically in the school again. The document that my father presented to the school was so well written that he had a clause giving him the right to collect the money awarded by the settlement if any of his demands were ever violated. My mother thought that the lawsuit would make it harder for our family to continue to live in the community, but in fact it gave my father a huge level of respect within the community especially from the poor families; my father became an instant hero. My sister's story shows that we all have the power to create systemic changes. We must create our own opportunities, and we must band together to put pressures on those who need to create change within the workforce for women, minorities, individuals with disabilities, and same sexual orientation. Someone said to me once in order to be oppressed, you must allow for someone else to oppress you. We, as a diverse community, have more economic, political power and influence than we think we have.

I will also share an example in this chapter of a lack of a systemic approach to diversity and inclusion to illustrate what happened to an organization that dismissed the impact of a systemic process of change.

I will break down each diverse group and show their statistical power and influence in the United States.

Women
Women forget at times the purchasing, workforce, and political powers they possess

- Women earn, spend, and influence spending at a greater rate than ever before, accounting for seven trillion dollars in consumer and business spending in the United States.

- Fifty-one percent of private wealth in the United States is controlled by women.

- Women account for over 50 percent of all stock ownership in the United States.

- Women control more than 60 percent of all personal wealth in the United States.[48]

- Women comprise 47 percent of the total US labor force.

- Women account for 51.5 percent of all workers in the high-paying management, professional, and related occupations.

---

[48] (http://www.askingsmarterquestions.com/marketing-to-women-surprising-stats-show-purchasing-power-influence/#sthash.PVAOeoDa.dpuf)

- Women are projected to account for 51 percent of the increase in total labor force growth between 2008 and 2018.[49]

- Fifty-six percent of women voted for President Obama in 2008, and 55 percent voted for him in 2012.

- Twenty women held US Senate seats in 2012.[50]

These statistics were very revealing when I first glanced at them; I felt that women should have more power and influence in this country, but this ideal is far from reality. I believe our biggest barrier is ourselves. We need to learn to negotiate our salaries, we need to learn to mentor other women and find mentors that will do the same for us; we *must* run for political office and encourage and support other women to run; we need to demand policy changes by getting involved with political action groups. We need to fight for women's rights and equality. We must demand to be heard. We need to use our purchasing power and political influence to demand change at all levels. We can use our purchasing power to demand that the companies that we use for services or investments have a portfolio of women in top management positions, as well as on their boards of directors and among their trustees, or we should boycott those organizations. We must always look for opportunities for other women without having a personal agenda. We must expect more from other women but expect even more from ourselves. We must help and support women who make it to the top so they can be successful. We must defend them, encourage them, and help them fight their battles. We must encourage our mothers, sisters, daughters, nieces, and granddaughters not to settle for less. They need to aim high and dream big. We must also be a true friend to other women and stop calling each other derogatory names, even in jest. People perceive us as others describe us. Stop putting other women down; be there to pick up the pieces when one of them falls, and be there when the best times are happening to celebrate with them. Let's stop being our own worst enemy and stop putting up barriers to other women who need our help.

Minorities

The US workforce is undoubtedly becoming more diverse. As of June 2012 people of color made up 36 percent of the labor force. Breaking it down by race and ethnicity, approximately 99,945,000 people (or 64 percent) in the labor force are non-Hispanic white; 24,679,000 (16 percent) are Hispanic;

---

[49] (Annual Averages: Employment and Earnings, January 2011)
[50] (Abdullah 2012)

18,758,000 (12 percent) are African American; and 8,202,000 (5 percent) are Asian. Approximately 4,801,000 people (3 percent) in the labor force do not identify in any of these racial or ethnic categories.

The proportion of people of color participating in the workforce will only increase as the United States becomes a more racially and ethnically diverse country. Census data tell us that by 2050 there will be no racial or ethnic majority in our country. Further, between 2000 and 2050, new immigrants and their children will account for 83 percent of the growth in the working-age population.[51]

The Selig Center for Economic Growth at the University of Georgia's Terry College of Business estimated that the economic influence of minorities has grown in the past twenty years. The purchasing power of blacks, Native Americans, and Asian Americans is 15.3 percent of the nation's total, up from 12.5 percent a decade earlier. Their combined purchasing power is estimated at $1.9 trillion.

At $1.2 trillion, US Hispanic purchasing power today is larger than the economies of all but 13 countries, said Jeff Humphreys, director of the Selig Center and author of the annual report "Multicultural Economy."

At the same time, online purchasing trends for all racial groups have increased in the past five years, according to a survey by the Media Audit, a Texas-based firm that tracks demographic online, radio, television, and online marketing trends. Surveys were conducted by phone five days a week, during the day and evening, selecting households using a random-digit dialing sample.

Between 2007 and 2012, blacks, Asians, and Latinos made the largest gains in online shopping. For example, blacks who purchased twelve or more items online in a single year increased to 18.7 percent in 2012, a 52 percent increase since 2007. During the same time, Hispanics who bought the same amount of goods via the Web accounted for 18.5 percent, a 45 percent increase.[52]

People with Disabilities
The employment-population ratio for persons with a disability was 17.8 percent in 2012, unchanged from 2011. The lower ratio among persons with a disability is due, in part, to the fact that a large share of the population of

---

[51] (The Employment Situation 2012)
[52] (Economic Growth 1990)

persons with a disability was age sixty-five and older, and older persons are less likely to be employed. However, across all age groups, persons with disabilities were much less likely to be employed than those with no disability.

Among persons with a disability age sixty-five and over, the employment-population ratio rose to 6.9 percent in 2012, while the ratio for persons age sixteen to sixty-four with a disability held at 27 percent.

In 2012, persons with a disability with higher levels of education were more likely to be employed than those with less education. At all levels of education, persons with a disability were much less likely to be employed than were their counterparts with no disability.

Workers with a disability were more likely than those with none to work part time. Among workers with a disability, 33 percent usually worked part time in 2012, compared with 19 percent of workers without a disability. The proportion of workers who were employed part time for economic reasons was slightly higher among those with a disability than among those without a disability (7 percent versus 6 percent). These individuals were working part time because their hours had been cut back or because they were unable to find a full-time job.

In 2012, workers with a disability were more likely than those with no disability to work in production, transportation, and materials-moving occupations (16 percent compared with 12 percent). Those with a disability were less likely than those with no disability to work in management, professional, and related occupations (32 percent compared with 38 percent).

The share of workers with a disability employed in federal, state, and local government (15 percent) was about the same as the share for those with no disability (14 percent). Workers with a disability were less likely than those with no disability to be employed in private, salaried jobs (73 percent versus 79 percent). The incidence of self-employment among workers with a disability was higher than among workers with no disability (11 percent versus 7 percent).[53]

Handicapitalism: It's a brand new term that describes what is behind a dawning realization in business: people with disabilities should not be viewed as charity cases or regulatory burdens, but rather as profitable marketing targets. Now, mainstream companies, from financial services to

---

[53] (http://www.bls.gov/news.release/disabl.nr0.htm)

cell phone makers, are going beyond what is mandated by law and rapidly tailoring products to attract them.

A new training video from Norwest Mortgage, Inc., a unit of Wells Fargo & Co. in Des Moines, Iowa, details a number of products it offers, including vehicle-conversion loans and home-modification loans designed especially for the disabled. The video, a call to arms for its sales force, offers a stark rationale: "Fact: People with disabilities have money!"

In 1995, according to census figures, there were about 48.5 million people age fifteen and older with disabilities in the United States, with annual discretionary Income totaling $175 billion. [54]

LGBTQ Population
As I continue to talk about power and influence from diverse groups. The political influence of LGBTQ in the United States continues to increase from the creation of the Society of Human Rights founded by Henry Gerber in Chicago in 1924 to the Senate vote 65–31 to repeal "Don't ask, Don't Tell" policy allowing gays and lesbians to serve openly in the military to the so-called "Defense of Marriage Act," or DOMA, which was passed in 1996 by Congress and signed into law by President Bill Clinton. Section three of DOMA was struck down by the US Supreme Court; it prevented the federal government from recognizing any marriages between gay or lesbian couples for the purpose of federal laws or programs, even if those couples are considered legally married by their home state. The other significant part of DOMA makes it so that individual states do not legally have to acknowledge the relationships of gay and lesbian couples who were married in another state. Only the section that dealt with federal recognition was ruled unconstitutional in June 2013. This effort shows how the political impact of a group can create a change in policy.

The other component of influence is the purchasing power of this population. With the Supreme Court rulings on DOMA and Proposition 8 in the books, marketers are now taking an even closer look at the growing influence of LGBTQ Americans, and not just in politics, but in terms of the market for consumer brands.

A new study from Experian Marketing Services notes that the number of Americans identifying as lesbian, gay, bisexual, or transgendered has

---

[54] (Harris 1999).

grown over the past decade, with 4.3 percent of the non-Hispanic adult population identifying as LGBTQ today, compared with 3.4 percent in 2006.

And these consumers are younger, are more tech savvy, create more affluent households, and spend more. In its 2013 LGBTQ Report, Experian says married gay men have the highest household income when compared with their heterosexual and lesbian counterparts. They also have the highest discretionary spending per capita, devoting $6,794 per capita annually to nonessentials, $753 more than what heterosexual men spend. Gay, lesbian, bisexual, and transgender Americans are "social connectors," "mobile professionals," and "mobirati" (cell-phone savvy). [55]

For years, brands like Subaru have marketed significantly to LGBTQ consumers. Gay and bisexual men, per the report, are more likely to be "practical drivers who place a higher value on comfort and function over performance, image or status when buying a vehicle." They are also more likely to be drivers "who see their vehicle as an extension of their identity and whose primary motivations when selecting a vehicle are image and status."

While more heterosexual women (38 percent) than lesbian and bisexual women (25 percent) are in the "practical drivers" area, that trend reverses with men.

The populations that band together and organize effectively for a common cause are those that can really impact policy and systemic changes. For example, consider the Latino population and the last two presidential elections in the United States. Their skillful way to organize and reach Latinos and non-Latinos to vote for the Democratic Party was uncanny. Their great efforts are what pushed the Republican Party to reconsider Latinos as a powerful voting force and to embrace that population is the "in" thing to do by coming together as a partisan group to create an immigration reform in order to legalize the eleven million undocumented Latinos that are in this country. [56]

For organizations to implement systemic change that includes diversity and inclusion regarding women, minorities, people with disabilities, and LGBTQ populations, the organizations must be willing to fight for these individuals' rights within the workforce. Their voices must be heard, and their skills and talents must be valued as integral components of an organization.

---

[55] (Greenberg 2013)
[56] (Census Bureau Data, April 2013)

Ignoring the Impact of Community Diversity at the Organizational Level

Most of you reading this chapter would probably agree that the information I have shown here makes a lot of sense in relation to diverse groups and how they impact all of us economically and politically. I would like to illustrate an example of what occurs when an organization ignores the impact of any of these groups.

Celebrity Chef Paula Deen and some of her staff were allegedly accused of making racial slurs and sexually offensive remarks to some of her former employees. In a matter of days, Mrs. Deen saw her empire crumbled and became a persona non grata within her network, her corporate partners, and her large number of followers. Mrs. Deen and her management and legal team did not realize that her empire had reached organizational-level standards. (This phenomenon happens often when a mom-and-pop entity becomes a big business or corporation.) At the organizational level conduct and behavior compliance related to diversity take on a distinct meaning because of the law, external customer base, and the relationship an enterprise has with other business partners. As I mentioned before, in this book the function of diversity as a systemic process of change is the smart behavioral approach to adopting to survive in a global economy. For instance, the Food Network and Walmart, among other companies, parted ways from Mrs. Deen, suspending their relationships pending an investigation of her actions as soon as the allegation hit the airways. These organizations didn't suspend Mrs. Deen because they thought it was the right thing to do; they did it because they understood their diverse customer base, and they could not afford to lose their business loyalty. This example illustrates why civic diversity is detrimental at the organizational level and why a systemic approach to inclusion is a matter of economic survival in the modern business world.

Chapter 11

Professional Development for the Success of a Systemic Process of Change

Professional development relates to the skills and knowledge an employee gains to optimize his or her personal development, job growth, and longevity within a company. My framework is effective because every employee is required to participate in the learning process of this work.

It is also important to highlight at the outset that professional development is only one component of a larger set of the systemic changes and interventions, but also extremely important to include, in order to ensure that organizational diversity is understood and practiced by all employees.

The first prong of my framework is called "employee awareness" or the "I" (see chapter on the Framework Prongs I and II). Through intentional professional development, employees at each level learn about the systemic process of diversity and inclusion, the responsibility to make it work, and how to practice and include in every facet of their everyday work. They now conceptualize why diversity and inclusion are part of what they do every time they come in contact with internal or external customers (see competencies chapter 5 on internal and external customers). The emphasis is not on a feeling of diversity but on a behavioral approach to staying employed and meeting the organizational bottom line.

Professional development is divided into different levels of skill sets. Each component of the curriculum addresses the diversity and inclusion responsibilities of each level of employee, organizational goals, as well as the strategic plan on diversity and inclusion for the organization.

Professional Development structure for Prong I

    I.   First level of employees—"Staying Employed"

    II.   Diverse Supplier Development—"Building a diverse vendor base"

    III.   Human Resources—Hiring Managers "Finding the talent"

    IV. Managers and Supervisors—" Retaining the workforce"

    V.   Directors—"Harvesting the talent. Selecting the Best"

    VI. VPs, CEOs, Board of Directors, Trustees.—"Growing and Developing the Business" (See chapter 2 on top management support.)

The professional development structure described previously will vary for educational, health, and nonprofit settings.

Staying Employed Curriculum: First line of employees
This curriculum directs employees to explore what diversity is as a behavioral approach to inclusion, and how their interactions affect those they come in contact with in the workplace. This section confirms that diversity and inclusion go beyond understanding race, ethnicity, gender, etc. It is everything one does when he or she comes in contact with another human being and how that interaction creates a positive or negative outcome when working together and meeting the organizational bottom line.

Building a Diverse Vendor Base Curriculum:
Procurement department
It is essential that the leadership team develop a diverse vendor goal for the organization. It is very difficult for the purchasing department to create a definite goal in most cases if one is not already set in place by the leadership team.

This section will explore organizational competencies and how they work in concert with the strategic plan for inclusion. The participant will be guided to develop innovative outreach strategies to build a healthy vendor base that will include mentoring, promoting, and grooming diverse vendors. They will explore why business fairs are old school, expensive, and ineffective.

The purchasing or procurement department is one of the most difficult departments to integrate in inclusion management in a systemic process of change, especially if purchasing is decentralized. Sometimes purchasing agents tend to limit the opportunities to diverse vendors. Building a diverse vendor portfolio takes time, commitment and accountability. It has been my experience that most organization leave the percentages of diverse vendor outreach to the purchasing department. In the inclusion revolution framework the percentage of diverse vendor outreach is designed by the top leadership team. Performance appraisal standards are developed to emphasize the accountability of the purchasing agents within the organization, and intentional mentoring and grooming opportunities are available to diverse vendors.

During this professional development phase the procurement department will learn strategies for outreach to vendors and for developing comprehensive bid packages, purchasing orders, compliance system follow up, bid point scale, good faith effort clauses, activity success reporting, and accountability standards to be followed by all buyers within the company.

Finding-the-Talent Curriculum: Human Resources and Hiring Managers
These individuals are crucial to all organizations because they are in charge of bringing the talent and building a healthy workforce.

In this part of the professional development spectrum the employees will learn different and new tactics to cultivate prospective employee leads, to seek diverse candidates, and to create a pool of the best and most qualified candidates for job openings. In order for the personnel in this department to be successful and effective, they must be involved in community associations that are multicultural, school related, and youth group events. They should be able to work nontraditional hours to be effective. This professional development session will explore why college fairs are old school, very expensive, and ineffective.

The hiring managers' portion of the professional development piece will also include the evaluation of unconscious biases and how the best and most qualified for the job is incorporated in the selection process.

Retaining-the-Workforce Curriculum: Managers and Supervisors

Managers and supervisors will study the impact of intentional purpose and how implicit or unconscious biases affect the way they deal with a diverse workforce. This group will spend time studying affinity and organizational and individual biases. The competencies used during this session of the professional development will explore the need to understand and deal with the different generations present within the workforce and offer suggestions for how to retain them by building a diverse style of management and supervision. This chapter provides an in-depth approach to the strategic planning of the organizational goals for diversity and inclusion.

Harvesting-the-Talent Curriculum: Selecting the Best Directors

Directors will learn the techniques to groom and nominate employees for promotional opportunities, projects, and important committees within the organization during this professional development session. These learning tools will be essential for directors to continue to retain diverse employees, as well as to promote a company of choice for diverse candidates to work at within the community.

Growing and Developing the Business:
VPs, CEOs, Board of Directors, Trustees

This curriculum will study diverse trends and how each impact and affect organizational goals.

Chapter 12

The Diversity and Inclusion Professional

To meet the needs of an increasingly diverse global market, organizations have developed executive positions to guide their diversity agendas, and the reality is that in order to implement a culture of inclusion, the whole organization must be committed and accountable for the success of inclusion instead of just one person or department.

A systemic process of change cannot be implemented at any organization unless the person hired to lead the effort has the full support of the leadership team, is part of the leadership team, and has the power to influence policy. The title of this person must reflect the commitment of the organization to diversity and inclusion.

The diversity and inclusion professional must be in a top level leadership role in the organization to send the message of commitment and support throughout the whole organization. This professional must understand how diversity and inclusion work and how they are implemented at the organizational level. Part of the interview process is to find out what type of diversity model the person has used to fulfill his or her duties. If the person has used civic diversity to implement change, the hiring committee should be warned that this person does not truly know how to implement a systemic process of change within the workforce. A person in this role who believes that diversity is a feeling and not a behavior is not the person to make an impact for your organization.

In the inclusion revolution framework, the diversity and inclusion professional needs to be a person that has an understanding of what cultural change means at the organizational level; is willing to learn the process to implement the change; and is given the resources and authority to hire consultants to assist in the process when necessary.

Diversity/Inclusion is an unexplored science that requires the attention to those that practice it.

Diversity and inclusion professionals are essential in leading my systemic process of change framework. It takes someone with the knowledge, education, leadership skills, and commitment to assist the leadership team in changing the culture of an organization.

Qualifications

- be able to understand, practice, and champion a systemic approach to diversity at the organizational level

- has the education, research background in diversity and inclusion management

- understand that diversity doesn't only impact a race or a group

- be open minded and willing to work with people from the different cultures

- be a good listener

- be able to convey to the leadership team and the staff that the position is the umbrella for the agenda of diversity but is not responsible for being the diversity person for all. This means that the person has to be able to be the one carrying out the diversity agenda but not the one that takes care of all diversity issues in a systemic process. In the systemic process, everyone is accountable for diversity and inclusion.

Duties

Diversity professionals are required to keep up on current Equal Opportunity and Affirmative Action regulations, as well as with common nondiscrimination policy. These individuals are often expected to be versatile employees, functioning with skills in areas such as human resources, administration, and management. They may need to mitigate diversity-based disputes and accusations of discrimination against the organization or other employees. Other duties could include the creation and promotion of diversity-oriented events, minority and protected class inclusion programs, and cross-cultural workshops. Occasionally, these professionals are called upon to produce best practices in diversity material, promoting inclusiveness, and ensuring continued compliance with government regulations.

Requirements
A diversity professional must be required to hold at least a bachelor's degree. A masters in diversity and inclusion studies recommended. The undergraduate degree programs must include business administration, human resources, and diversity management classes. Classes in cultural diversity will teach students how to function within a diverse workforce and how to promote cultural inclusion in a variety of professional environments. There are also several types of diversity professional certificates available from different organizations and universities around the country. I also offer a certificate for those who would like to become an expert on my inclusion revolution framework.

Typical Work Activities
The work carried out by equality and diversity professionals may differ slightly depending on the area in which they specialize, but in general typical activities are likely to include the following:

- compliments everyone in the organization in their efforts to promote inclusion management

- researches, applies, and promotes diversity systemic processes and shares best practices

- provides advice, guidance, and support on all equality and diversity issues

- assesses community needs and promoting community cohesion

- works hand in hand with the leadership to develop diversity strategic plan components

- assists in promoting changes within organizations and the wider community

- develops systems for reporting any incidents of discrimination

- liaises with community groups and other relevant organizations, e.g. police, local councils, etc.

- assists in raising awareness in schools, colleges and the wider community

- works with management in teaching them how to deal with diversity and conflicts within the workplace

- interacts with people at all levels and from a wide variety of backgrounds

- assists in responding to complaints and providing information on options for complainants

- translates equality legislation into practice to ensure organizations meet statutory requirements

- ensures Equality Impact Assessments are carried out

- writes, implements, and reviews policy at corporate and service level to embed within wider strategic plans

- assists the leadership team set targets and/or action plans and monitoring progress

- develops links with key professional bodies

- represents the organization on regional and national forums and working groups

- oversees and monitoring staff recruitment including diverse populations, and staff development

- assists in preparing and delivering presentations and workshops to staff, stakeholders and partner organizations

The organizations that have made a commitment to diversity and inclusion and are excellence driven will have money allocated to pay for this position, and the salary is commensurate with experience. The person is part of the top leadership team like a vice president or above, and has the VP's support, has power, and has great influence on policy and a strong voice on the development of the diversity strategic plan.

Note: Hire the diversity and inclusion professional in what the person brings to the organization to compliment or create a systemic process of change. Being from a culture of difference doesn't necessary make a person more suitable to lead this position. It has taken me years of research, and field experiences to become an expert on the Latino cultures and a specialist in systemic processes of change regarding diversity and inclusion at the organizational level.

Chapter 13

Accountability

The most constant element in an organization is change. Change is sometimes the hardest element to implement regarding diversity and inclusion. The organizational diversity framework that I have been describing in this book is one of those systemic processes of change that have such a positive outcome because it is the first time that management and employees understand what diversity and inclusion mean in the workplace. Secondly, management and employees understand how the inclusion management competencies are used to explain in a very clear format what behaviors are expected from the each other to continue to be employed; and next the element of my framework that I am going to share with you is accountability and why is one of the most crucial and essential element in creating a culture of inclusion at the organizational level.

Accountability
Webster's Dictionary defines accountability as "an obligation or willingness to accept responsibility or to account for one's actions." This definition is so insightful because it reflects the behavioral component of my framework. Diversity and inclusion are only present if everyone within the organization practices the behaviors set forth by its competencies and accountability. Accountability without metrics is just half of the equation. In addition to the metrics, an emphasis should be put on broadcasting successes, and rewards must be based on the cultural changes created by the paradigm shift at the organizational level. Companies sometimes fail to make the direct connection from accountability to diversity standards instead of using the organization needs to make a commitment to engage employees and management at all levels; all these groups must practice the behaviors of inclusion if they wish to continue to work for the organization. Organization's

goals to align diversity and inclusion with the business mission and strategic plan of the organization.

A well-defined performance appraisal can be one of those vehicles that I recommend to help each employee be more accountable. For instance, as you are reading this chapter you may say, "Our company already has diversity standards reflected on our employees' performance appraisals." Most of the diversity standards that I have reviewed for companies are so vague and scored so low that the employees don't feel a responsibility or a commitment to implement diversity and inclusion practices. Strong diversity accountability standards must be designed to successfully implement my systemic process of change.

Diversity standards must incorporate qualitative metrics that have an immediate impact, are measurable, and get at the behavioral changes and outcomes the company wants. These must include good faith efforts to build a diverse and inclusive workplace. There are a couple of standards that I recommend you add to your performance appraisals, and which sometimes get omitted from the standards. Assess the retention of diverse employees within the employee's department and potential diverse population referral by each employee. The standards for management need to include a number of diverse mentees per year, hiring turnover, and promotion of diverse employees within his or her department.

It is amazing how rapidly the behavior of the leadership team and employees can shift when the accountability standards are linked with a scorecard. It must be noted that in order to impact cultural behavioral changes at a higher level within an organization, a significant percentage of bonuses and raises should be closely connected with the implementation and practice of inclusion. I recommend 25 to 35 percent of the total raise or bonus to really create an impact and to send a message to the workforce that the organization is committed and serious about creating a culture of inclusion. When employees actively practice accountability in the workplace, they tend to feel more pride and ownership in the company. Managers, however, must set the stage for this to happen by treating all employees as valued members of a team who each have an integral role in helping the company achieve its goals. According to the Ethics Center for Engineering and Research, when employees feel pride in their place of employment because of the accountability and integrity practiced throughout the organization, they are more likely to work efficiently, reduce risks, and have better loss control.[57]

Assessment and Evaluation

One cannot develop a successful diversity process without ongoing assessment and evaluating the status and accomplishments of the process. Although the frequency may vary, world class diversity organizations make assessing and evaluating their diversity process an integral part of their management system. Diversity measures include:

- employee attrition rates;

- workforce satisfaction;

- market share within new customer bases;

- external awards and recognition for diversity efforts; and

- workplace climate satisfaction.

Accountability is extremely important in the implementation of systemic change regarding diversity and inclusion. If we don't make each employee responsible for his or her actions and make a commitment to create a climate of inclusion, how will tangible change be created? It takes the participation of all of the employees to work together to meet the organizational goals.

---

[57] (http://www.ehow.com/info_7854666_importance-accountability-integrity-workplace.html#ixzz2WgGWSZTh)

Chapter 14

Best Practices for Diversity and Inclusion

One of the major stumbling blocks in discussions surrounding diversity is its very definition. For our purposes, we use the following definition of diversity: diversity includes all characteristics and experiences that define each of us as individuals. A common misconception about diversity is that only certain persons or groups are included under its umbrella, when in fact, exactly the opposite is true. Diversity includes the entire spectrum of dimensions of an individual, including race, ethnicity, gender, age, religion, disability, and sexual orientation (referred to as *REGARDS*). Secondary dimensions commonly include: communication style, work style, organizational role/level, economic status, and geographic origin (e.g., East, Midwest, and South). It is a simple fact that each of us possesses unique qualities affected by each of these dimensions. Experience and recent research indicate that when recognized and valued, diversity enhances individual productivity, organizational effectiveness, and sustained competitiveness.[58]

In order "to maximize the utilization of its human capital, organizations must go beyond merely creating a more diverse workplace. Once there, the value of having diverse employees must be recognized."[59] Now is the time to move beyond viewing diversity as merely the numerical representation of certain groups. It is time for a systematic application of diversity concepts to the business of the organization. Aligning diversity with the mission and business of the organization increases employee satisfaction and

---

[58] (Taylor, Cultural Diversity in Organizations 1994)
(Morrison, 1992)
[59] (Renae, 1997)

retention; improves competitiveness and productivity; increases responsiveness; and adds value to the customer. Best practices include those tools that can help the organization continue to move forward, measure its success and failure, and help the organization continue to reevaluate and improve in its attempts for inclusion. Most research that looks at systemic changes for diversity identifies the following best practices:

1. Leadership and management commitment—See chapter 2

2. Employee involvement

3. Strategic planning

4. Diversity indicators—See chapter on accountability

5. Accountability, measurement, and evaluation—See chapter on accountability

Employment Involvement

As I explained previously, diversity and inclusion are the responsibility of every employee; it goes beyond a person or department. Because of this dynamic, management recognizes the importance of employee involvement in the process of change. They also recognize that being competitive in a global economy requires the full utilization of the skills and talents of all employees to better serve their customers, to increase employee satisfaction, and to meet the needs of diverse communities. So, in an organization where the employees are allowed to be part of the systemic change by having a voice in the process, the transition to inclusion is easier to attain than when employees are told to believe in diversity without understanding why.

The United State Department of Commerce suggests different ways employees can be involved in a systemic process of change.

• An upper level leadership team that guides and evaluates the company's progress toward achieving its diversity goals. The team gains insights from an advisory group that represents eight employee councils. Each employee council has a corporate vice president as a sponsor. The councils are inclusive—anyone who wants to promote cross-cultural communication is encouraged to become involved.

• To institutionalize diversity management at a one-partner organization, individuals who are seen as potential leadership successors are asked to become champions of diversity before assuming a leadership role.

Once they become leaders they are already established as proponents of diversity.

• One partner recognizes the contributions of its managers to advancing diversity. For example, in 1998 it created a Chief Executive Officer/ Chief Operating Officer Diversity Award. This award recognizes managers whose commitment to diversity makes them role models for others. Such champions are used to share their experiences throughout the company to demonstrate the benefit of diversity to others.[60]

Affinity Groups

Affinity groups are small groups of people who support each other and work together for a common goal. These groups provide a forum to both articulate and understand the varied needs and interests of employees. Participation in these groups is welcomed. Often, input is sought from employee groups to determine their perception of progress achieved with regard to diversity.

Diversity Councils

Diversity councils represent a cross section of the organization's workforce. A skills and talent grid of all of the characteristics desired as well as REGARDS for this council is used to ensure diversity within this body.

Diversity Strategic Planning

Strategic planning for diversity focuses on creating measurable ways that diversity can support the strategic direction, goals, and objectives of the organization.[61] Strategic-level, long-range planning for diversity is a more recent development. Previously, diversity was not seen as an integral part of strategic planning. Diversity initiatives were often poorly conceptualized, lacked specificity, and were not linked to strategic organizational plans. Today's leaders realize that in order to be effective, successful diversity planning must be aligned with and provide support for strategic business objectives and operational decisions.

Dr. David Kelly from Stanford University is the founder of IDEO and creator of the Human Center of Behavior Design. What made me study his work is his ability to bring people from all walks of life together to develop a product. These talented individuals are free to express their thoughts,

---

[60] (Reinvesting Government Benchmarking Study, Sep. 28, 2011)
[61] (Hubbard, Measuring Diversity Results)

concerns, and ideas, and the outcome of the dialogue creates magnificent products. Organizational diversity works well and is so effective because it makes organizations aware of the talents and skills that their diverse employees bring to achieve the organization's goals. Best practice is a conduit to success for diverse organizations that incorporate systemic changes to accomplish inclusion.

Chapter 15

A Systemic Approach to Diversity and Inclusion at Its Best

I developed the inclusion revolution framework in 2008, but I have been doing research and field work on the subject since 1999. I worked with different sized companies, but for this book I needed a large corporation that was looking for a change in diversity and inclusion practices. I also wanted a company that had union and non-union employees, preferably in a male-dominated industry. I also was looking for an organization that had at least 1,000 employees. Happily, I was able to find such a corporation among my clientele. The particular corporation that I used serves three different states and has a workforce over 1,500 employees.

As I embarked in this process of change with this organization, I was able to confirm some essential elements that were already in place. First, the president and the leadership team were on board. Second, this group already had organizational competencies in place, but they had never been used in inclusion management to make employees aware or accountable for inclusion. Third, the organization had a strategic plan, but the leadership team was working in modifying it to reflect diversity and inclusion as I entered my contract with them.

I was asked by the diversity manager to put together a pilot program for a group of employees. My pilot was a tremendous success, and after my first presentation the diversity manager told me that he saw a transformation among the participants he had never before witnessed during a diversity training or presentation. After my initial pilot session, I was offered a contract with this very progressive organization.

The tangible changes I observed in this organization during the implementation of the first prong of my framework were numerous:

1. Intentional purpose was implemented in the recruitment, hiring, and promotion of diverse job candidates and employees.

2. The company's diversity council was revived and became very functional in diversity and inclusion outreach and resources.

3. A multicultural library was developed for employees who wanted to know more about diversity and inclusion.

4. All employees were required to attend professional development sessions to learn about the inclusion revolution framework and how to use it at work.

5. The sense of diversity as a feeling was no longer the mind-set of the employees.

6. Grooming and mentoring became intentional by upper management and was practiced consistently.

7. Some minority employees were promoted to managerial positions.

8. The intentional goal of hiring diverse employees was met.

Employees Testimonial:

- "Maura was engaging and did not infuse her personal beliefs—as previous trainers have done. I think, after thirty years in [the] workforce, [it was the] best diversity session I've had."

- "I was able to understand how diversity applies to me in the workplace."

- "Thank you for not making the training a black thing. My coworkers always think that is because of me that we are having diversity training."

- "I really like how Maura used company's competencies to help me understand how diversity and inclusion is everyone's responsibility"

- "This approach helped me understand that the way I feel about diversity on my own time is my own personal concern, but how I treat and work with others is what is most important in making people feel welcome and accepted."

- "I wanted to be sure to send a note to tell you how much I appreciated the diversity training provided by Maura Robinson. She is not only a terrific person to work with, her knowledge and presentation style were excellent. It was so easy to learn and participate. Her presentation was unique and refreshing. The approach was logical and easy to embrace."

- "This was an excellent experience. As a manager, I was glad to know that unconscious biases do affect how we treat employees. The exercise was eye opening to me."

- "I understand now how diversity and getting along and working with others is my responsibility. I thought that diversity was a feeling, and now that I know it is a behavior. I will be more aware of my actions when interacting with my employees and coworkers."[62]

This corporation is one of those organizations that understands, believes, and has an ongoing thirst for making diversity and inclusion part of the tapestry of the organization. The leadership is committed to making this organization the ideal place for employment. My framework creates systemic tangible changes when implementing diversity and inclusion in the workplace.

---

[62] (Robinson M., 2012–2013)

Conclusion

Minorities, classified as those of any race other than non-Hispanic, single-race whites, currently constitute about a third of the US population, according to 2010 census figures. But by 2042, they are projected to become the majority, making up more than half the population. By 2050, 54 percent of the population will be minorities. Minority children are projected to reach that milestone even sooner. With this type of information one would tend to believe that disparities within the workplace would diminish, but the reality of the matter is that minorities and individuals from the culture of difference are still lagging behind in the workforce. As long as corporations continue to think of diversity as a feeling, a thing, a person, a department, an initiative, or a program minorities, women, people with disabilities, and GLBTQ people will never be able to have a fair opportunity for hiring and promotion at the organizational level.

This book defined what diversity and inclusion meant at the organizational level, how a system process of change is created, and how cultural competencies of success can be incorporated into every facet of an organization to promote inclusion and meet the organization's bottom line.

The Inclusion Revolution is Now offers a systemic process for change that has never been utilized before at the organizational level. It offers a behavioral approach to change by holding every individual within the organization accountable for his or her actions. This systemic process of change moves from a *feeling* of diversity that doesn't have a lasting impact, to a tangible, behavioral approach to change that is concrete and everlasting.

A systemic approach to diversity and inclusion is the only way to ensure that the disproportionate number of minorities, women, and people from cultures of difference is balanced within the workforce.

A systemic process for incorporating diversity and inclusion takes time to implement. As you learned in this book, having a champion in leadership during this process is essential and a strong diversity and inclusion strategic plan is a must. The right team is essential to help implement the message, which may have to include a consultant that is trained and certified in the inclusion revolution framework to get the organization on board. A logic model is one vehicle to help implement an effective process at the organizational level. Performance appraisal standards on diversity and inclusion must also be incorporated and communicated to each employee; accountability is the weapon of success. Inclusion management competencies are so essential for creating behavioral changes within the workforce. These competencies work as the foundational structure of the message and as a strategic plan. But most of all, the understanding and utilization of diversity and inclusion best practices becomes ingrained in employees' minds as they interact with each other in the workplace.

I hope my book inspires you to become a pioneer in your organization and community and to create a positive transformation that will benefit people that have been under represented at the organizational level. It is through employment and job opportunities that minorities, women, and people from cultures of difference will excel and be able to share wealth, educate themselves, their children, and prepare for a healthy tomorrow.

I wish you well in this wonderful journey. Please visit my website at www. mgrobinsoninc.com for consultation, speaking engagements, working partnership opportunities, and information on certification in my inclusion revolution framework.

Works Cited

http://www.askingsmarterquestions.com/marketing-to-women-surprising-stats-show-purchasing-power-influence/#sthash.PVAOeoDa.dpuf. (n.d.).

http://www.askingsmarterquestions.com/marketing-to-women-surprising-stats-show-purchasing-power-influence/#sthash.PVAOeoDa.dpuf. (n.d.).

http://www.bls.gov/news.release/disabl.nr0.htm. (n.d.). Bureau of Labor Statistics.

http://www.ehow.com/info_7854666_importance-accountability-integrity-workplace.html#ixzz2WgGWSZTh. (n.d.).

Ross, Howard. 2008. "Proven Strategies for Addressing Unconscious Bias in the Workplace." *CDO Insight* 2 (5), 09-24.

Mottershead, T. 2008. *The Art and Science of Talent.* California: Korn/Ferry.

Taylor, J. 2011. "Persistent Racial Inequalities." *Economist's View.* February 4. http://economistsview.typepad.com/economistsview/2011/02/persistent-racial-inequalities.html.

AARP. 2003. "Staying Ahead of the Curve." *The AARP Working in Retirement Study.* Washington, DC.

Abdullah, H. 2012. *How Women Ruled the 2012 Election and Where the GOP Went Wrong.* November 8, 2012.

Allen, J. 2008. "Wellness leadership." *Healthy Cultures*: 1–12.

Banaji, M. R. 1991. "Measuring Unconscious Attitude." *The Ontario Symposium 7*: 55–76.

Berry, J. 1993. "Ethnic Identity in Plural Societies." In *Ethnic Identity: Formation and Transmission among Hispanics and Other Minorities*, edited by Martha E. Bernal, 271–296. Albany, NY: SUNY Press.

Brown, R., et al. 2005. "An Integrative Theory of Intergroup Contact." *Advances in Experimental Social Psychology* 37: 205, 255–343.

Career Advisory Board. 2011. *The Future of Millennial Careers.* Chicago, Il: DeVry University.

Collins, J. A. 1994. *Built to Last: Successful Habits of Visionary Companies.* New York, NY: Harper Business.

Cox, T. J. 1991. "Managing Cultural Diversity: Implications for Organizational Competitiveness." *Academy of Management Executive* 5: 45–56.

Cox, T. J. 1993. "Cultural Diversity in Organizations." *Theory, Research, and Practice*, 1–7.

Cox, T. J. 1991. "Models of Acculturation for Intra-organizational Cultural diversity." *Canada Journal of Administrative Sciences* 8: 90–100.

Ferdman, B. M. 2004. "The Inclusive Workplace." In *Managing a Diverse Workforce*, edited by G. N. Powell, 165–168. Thousand Oaks, CA: Sage Publications.

Ferdman, B. M. 1995. "Bridging the Gap between Group Differences and Individual Uniqueness." *Cultural Identity and Diversity Organizations,* edited by M. M. Chemers et al., 37–61. Thousand Oaks, CA: Sage Publications.

Gardenswartz, L. et al. 1993. *Managing Diversity: A Complete Desk Reference and Planning Guide.* Burr Ridge, IL: McGraw-Hill.

Gilgoff, D. 2009. "Breaking the Corporate Glass Ceilings." *USNews.* November 20.

Glynn, S. J. 2013. Women's Economic Policy Center for American Progress. 1–5.

Greenberg, K. 2013. "LGBTQ Market is Affluent and Influential." *Marketing Daily,* June, 2013..

GreenBook the guide for marketing. n.d. In r. http://www.greenbook.org/marketing-research.cfm/millennial-cause-study.

Hamel, G. A. 1994. *Competence-Based Competition.* New York: Wiley & Sons.

Hecht, H. L. 1994. "Leadership Development: After Downsizing." *Career Transition,* 3–15. Perseus Publishing.

Horsch, K. 1997. "Indicators: Definition and Use in a Results-Based Accountability System." *Harvard Family Research Project,* 1–55.

Hubbard, E. E. 1997. *Measuring Diversity Results.* Petaluma, CA: Global Insights.

Jackson S. E., and Alavarez, E. B. 1992. "Working through Diversity as a Strategic Imperative." *Diversity in the Workplace: Human Resources Initiative,* 13–29. New York: The Guilford Press.

Judge, T. A. 2004. "The Effect of Physical Height on Workplace Success and Income." *Journal of Applied Psychology* June, 428.

Kansas, t. U. (n.d.). *The Community Tool Box is a service of the Work Group for Community Health and Development.* Kansas. AU: The Community Tool Box Organization.

Katz, J. et al. 1994. *The Promise of Diversity.* New York: McGraw-Hill.

Kellogg Foundation, W. K. 2004. Logic Model Guide. January, 7–33.

Kersten, D. 2002. "Today's Generations Face New Communications Gap." *USA Today*, November 15.

Lawler, E. I. 1995. "The New Pay: A Strategic Approach." *Compensation & Benefits Review* July/August, 14–22.

Ledford, G. J. 1995a. "Designing Nimble Reward Systems." *Compensation & Benefits Review* July/August, 46–54.

Ledford, G. J. 1995b. "Paying for the Skills, Knowledge, and Competencies of Knowledge Workers." *Compensation and Benefits Review* 27: 55–62.

Miller, F. A. 1994. "Forks in theRroad: Critical Issues on the Path to Diversity."

Morrison, A. M. 1992. *The New Leaders: Guidelines on Leadership Diversity in America.* San Francisco: Josey Bass.

Norton, J. R. 1997. *The Change Equation.* City: Press.

Pew Hispanic Center. 2013. "Census Bureau Data."

Praeger, J. H. 1999. "People with Disabilities are the Next Consumer Niche." *The Wall Street Journal*, December 15.

Ramarajan, L. S. 2008. "The Influence of Organizational Respect on Emotional Exhaustion in the Human Services." *Journal of Positive Psychology* 3: 4–18.

Robinson, M. 2000. "Visible Diversity." *NAWBO*,1–10. Indianapolis, IN: NAWBO.White Paper

Robinson, M. 2012–2013. *The Inclusion Revolution, Prong I, Professional Development Survey 1675 Employees.* Evansville, IN: M. G. Robinson, Inc.

Robinson, M. G. 2000. "Organizational Diversity, the Only Solution to Inclusion in the Workplace." *The New Way of Doing Business.* Lafayette, IN: Rowman & Littlefield.

Robinson, M. G. 2000. The Inclusion Revolution Framework. January. White paper

Rowe, M. 2008. "Micro-affirmations and Micro-inequities." *Journal of the International Ombudsman Association* 1 (1):112-134.

Russell Sage Foundation. 1990. *Multi-City Study of Urban Inequality.* http://www.russellsage.org/research/multi.

Selig, Simon S., Jr. Center for Economic Growth, University of Georgia. 1990. *Economic Growth.*

Smiley, L. 2013. *A Generation Divided over Diversity.* University of California Press.

Solomon, E. J. 1993. Recognizing Resistance: Creating Readiness for Organization Change. *Diversity Factor* 1: 16–20.

Taylor, S. C. 1994. *Cultural Diversity in Organizations.* San Francisco: Berrett-Koehler.

US Department of Commerce. 2011. *Reinvesting Government Benchmarking Study.* September 28.

US Department of Labor, Bureau of Labor Satistics. 2011. *Annual Averages: Employment and Earnings.*

US Department of Labor, Bureau of Labor Statistics. 2012. *The Employment Situation.* June.

Watson, T. 2011–2012. "Clear Direction in a Complex World." 1: 2–30.

About the Author

Maura G. Robinson is a sociologist with a master's degree in public administration. Her company, M. G. Robinson, Inc., specializes in organizational development in the area of diversity and inclusion. An expert on gender issues and generational trends and behaviors, she has taught part time at the University of Evansville for twenty-four years and writes a column on Latino issues for *El Informador Latino*, a local newspaper. She lives in Indiana.

Open Book Editions
A Berrett-Koehler Partner

Open Book Editions is a joint venture between Berrett-Koehler Publishers and Author Solutions, the market leader in self-publishing. There are many more aspiring authors who share Berrett-Koehler's mission than we can sustainably publish. To serve these authors, Open Book Editions offers a comprehensive self-publishing opportunity.

A Shared Mission

Open Book Editions welcomes authors who share the Berrett-Koehler mission—Creating a World That Works for All. We believe that to truly create a better world, action is needed at all levels—individual, organizational, and societal. At the individual level, our publications help people align their lives with their values and with their aspirations for a better world. At the organizational level, we promote progressive leadership and management practices, socially responsible approaches to business, and humane and effective organizations. At the societal level, we publish content that advances social and economic justice, shared prosperity, sustainability, and new solutions to national and global issues.

Open Book Editions represents a new way to further the BK mission and expand our community. We look forward to helping more authors challenge conventional thinking, introduce new ideas, and foster positive change.

For more information, see the Open Book Editions website:
http://www.iuniverse.com/Packages/OpenBookEditions.aspx

Join the BK Community! See exclusive author videos, join discussion groups, find out about upcoming events, read author blogs, and much more! http://bkcommunity.com/

Made in the USA
Lexington, KY
21 August 2015